THE EXPERIMENT IS OVER

**"Planet Earth is about to be upgraded.
It is time to awaken to who you are
and where you came from."**

PAUL G. LOWE

Edited by
Roxi McNay

D1343091

The Roximillion Publications Corporation
New York

The Roximillion Publications Corporation
1202 Lexington Avenue, Suite 325
New York NY 10028

Photographs by: Sandy Kaplin, Sahyma Lach-
mann, Rene Minosa, Maryanne Russell.

Manufactured in United States of America

The publisher wishes to convey his gratitude to everyone who has contributed to producing this book, including:

> Phoenicia Graham
> Aurora Terry
> Dries van Wagenberg
> Kyala Sanati Zacharias
> All members of the Six–Month and Six–Weeks Projects transcription teams.

THE EXPERIMENT IS OVER

CONTENTS

Chapter Fifteen – Living Consciously / 212

An Interview by Monny Curzon

The only way to affect anything globally, if anything can be affected on such a large scale, is through the individual. That supreme energy that has been called God is in everyone, now.

Chapter Sixteen – Meditation / 229

An Interview by Phoenicia Graham

Meditation isn't anything, just sit and watch what happens. When you have a thought, you are aware of having that thought; when you have a feeling, you are aware of having that feeling. If you are disturbed, you are aware of being disturbed, you don't do anything about it. You just watch. Choicelessly.

Chapter Seventeen – The Art Of Seeing / 243

An Interview by Velusia

Everything that is contained in each universe is contained within each being. It is not that God is within, each person is God, now. And they have never not been.

Chapter Eighteen – Being Yourself / 256

An Interview by Salila

The only thing we need to do is to feel who we are in each moment. We can become sensitive to whatever is happening rather than contracting away from it. If we experience the layers and layers of ourselves, we reach the place of light and purity.

Editor's Introduction

On September I 1987, The Six Month Project started in a large villa overlooking Lago Maggiore in Northern Italy. The project was directed by Paul Lowe and involved sixty people living together for six months, with the goal of self–realization.

I was one of those sixty people and it was by far the most intense six months of my life. The participants came from thirteen different countries, their ages ranged from twenty–two to sixty–three, and they were from all walks of life – students, actors, businessmen, housewives, architects, therapists, nearly as many occupations as people. Everyone who was there went through a dramatic transformation, and in itself the Six Months Project is worthy of a book. Maybe someone will write it one day.

During that time, Paul spoke to the group at least once a day, and hundreds of hours of tapes were recorded. This book contains some of the most important interviews conducted with him during that time, and during a later six–week seminar directed by him held in Southern Germany in March and April 1988. In the book there are also four interviews done after that period, two in France and two in the United States.

Members of the Six Month Project are now living and working all over the world. So much happened for so many people. The process has continued for all those involved, and in many cases people have moved far beyond the stage they had reached when these interviews took place. Many are now leading their own seminars, and at the same time, are still continuing to learn and grow.

This book was transcribed, edited and assembled in the United States during the late summer and autumn of 1988.

Each chapter in essence contains the same message: *We are not who we think we are, we are much, much more.*

It doesn't contain a blueprint for realization or exercises or a plan of action. It does contain many suggestions. Each individual's path is different, our hindrance is what we think we know, not what we don't know.

Paul and I would love to hear from you if you have anything to say about the book. Much has happened for me during the time I spent working on it. Often, when something was happening in me, I would come across the perfect passage to read, and then suddenly everything was different. So, do let us know what happens for you when you read it.

I hope you enjoy it!

Roxi McNay

PAUL G. LOWE

Paul Graham Lowe was born at approximately 12:50 p.m. on March 16, 1933, in Warwickshire, England. His father, Walter, was a cap maker at that time, his mother, Elsie, a very devoted and caring housewife. Two brothers Clive and David, were later born into the family and there developed a very close connection between them all.

Paul spent much of his childhood alone, roaming around the countryside near his home. He had an excellent singing voice and, when he was seven years old, he joined the local church choir. Giles of England. He became the choir leader, and spent much of his time singing. In his teens, most of his spare time was spent bicycling – riding about one thousand miles per month.

He left school at fourteen with the minimum education. Paul attended many extra–mural education courses but, after a time, realized that for him experience was more valuable than conventional education. His first job was in a stockbrokers in Birmingham. He was to have many occupations – salesman, sales representative, interior designer, photographer none of them for longer than two years.

In 1956, he married Mavis Harris. The marriage was very loving, but Paul wanted to explore the world, so in 1964 they parted amicably and he set off to hitch–hike around the world. On his way, he met Patricia Clare Soloway with whom he shared many adventures and who eventually became his second wife, and mother of his two children – Tania and Ryan.

The next six years were spent in a variety of situations around the world. In East Africa, he managed the Y.M.C.A. hotel in Nairobi, was a field worker for the Red Cross, and managed the Kenya Charity Fundraising Organization. In Hong Kong, he became the senior account manager for the advertising agency that handled the colony's largest account. In 1968, when he read about Esalen and the Human Potential Movement, he immediately resigned his position and left for America. For the next twelve months he worked and studied with most of the foremost group leaders at that time.

In 1969, he returned to England and, with his wife Patricia, founded Quaesitor, a growth center, that was the first outside America and which over the next three years, was to become the second largest such center in the world. During this time, he introduced most of the well–known American group leaders to England, helped to found the Association of Humanistic Psychology in England, innovated many new experiential techniques, and trained group leaders, who later opened up Growth Centers all over Europe.

Late in 1972, he went to India to seek meditation techniques that would be suitable or adaptable to Western people. On this trip he was initiated by an Indian guru, and spent the next thirteen years in spiritual ashrams in India, and in other parts of the world. In this time he studied Eastern philosophy and religion, edited spiritual books, organized meditation camps, and developed many highly successful experimental techniques that combined awakening methods from the East and West. His encounter groups became legendary. He led many training courses and guided workshops that had up to five thousand participants. In 1981, he went on a world tour and held workshops for many thousands of people.

Late in 1985, he completed his association with spiritual ashrams and went to a large villa on the shores of Lake Maggiore, in Northern Italy, to supervise the forming of the International Academy of Meditation. There, another level of realization occurred, and a new phase of his work emerged which went beyond methods and techniques. This culminated in an intense six month experimental training course, designed to help participants to be available to very high levels of consciousness. Over sixty people participated in this experience, which was based in various formless meditations, honesty, and living choicelessly in each moment.

In 1988, Paul dissolved the academy and embarked on another world tour to make himself available in every way to meet and share his insight with crystalized and influential people who may be ready to be part of a transformational change on the planet.

For the past few months, he has been in retreat. He is now available again to speak at conferences and seminars. He has no permanent home or base, and lives his life as an availability, going wherever his work leads.

CHAPTER ONE

THE EXPERIMENT IS OVER

An Interview by Roxi McNay

Roxi: There is an age old question which has been asked as far back as history books and religious records go, and that is: Where do we come from?

Paul: The question can't be answered in this dimension. In this dimension, on planet Earth, where you and I can see each other now, we use words which are formed by the mind. The mind cannot understand what could be called the answer to this question. There isn't actually an answer. There is a knowingness, but there is not an answer as you know it. It is not possible to formulate what you call an answer in this dimension to something that is in another dimension. I think it is Lao Tzu who said, "The truth cannot be said. If it is said, it is not the truth."

We get very frustrated about that because in our arrogance we think we know every thing, and if we don't we can work it out or we can calculate it. And that is true, but not in this dimension. We have to leave this dimension in order to know that. Another way of trying to explain it is, if you have got one system of mathematics, you can't use that system to understand another system of mathematics.

The answer to your question is in a different language, it is a different dimension, a different vibration. What I do is I make up a story which is not true but is around the truth. The only way you can understand the truth is to let go of this dimension, which you do in meditation or in times of great stillness, then you become aware of other levels of vibration, other dimensions.

The story I make up about it is based on what all the stories are based on, the Adam and Eve story, the big bang theory. They are all around the truth, but none of them is the truth.

Another person who talked about it was Buddha and he said something like this, "Out of the whole came the whole and the whole remained." The big bang theory explains that there was one and then it exploded. We can look at it this way. There was one but it wasn't material, it wasn't solid, there wasn't one big planet or one big sun or one big anything. There was consciousness and we could call that God, but not God as a person, God as a vibration. And in this consciousness we became conscious that we were automatically conscious and not consciously conscious.

We were the one but we didn't appreciate the one. If you have only seen light, you can't appreciate light until you see darkness, and then when you see darkness the contrast shows you light and then you can appreciate the light. We were the one and we didn't appreciate ourselves, so we got this idea of disintegrating the one and finding out what it's like not to be in the one so we can appreciate the one. We can call it the big bang plus. There was a big bang and the one disintegrated into billions and billions of parts. The one still remained and that is what the mind has difficulty with. How can something be and not be at the same time? I have no way of explaining that to you in this dimension. The one disintegrated into billions of parts and the one also remained. Each of those billions of parts was the one, total and complete.

When this disintegration took place, it decided to forget that, so each of those billion parts was total and complete and the whole in itself, but it went to sleep to that, in order to have the fun and the experience of working its way back to full consciousness again.

We decided on Planet Earth what was probably one of the most difficult parts. We made a decision to create this planet through vibrational levels by having a thought. Thought is a vibration, it can move mountains, it can create and disintegrate things. It is a well–known phenomenon that there are people on the planet who can bend metal and do many other similar things with thought. So we decided to hold a thought, stabilize its vibrations, and let the vibrations lower themselves. As they did, they came together into something that we call material. This gives the impression of being solid, although through an electron microscope it can be seen that it is not. It is a movement of particles, and the particles aren't solid either, but they give an impression of being so.

We created this dimension in order to experience, not to think, not to intellectualize, but to experience duality. So we took the One and we dualized it into things like men and women, right and wrong, good and bad, benefit and harm, and light and darkness. We dichotomized everything and then we experienced this. We experienced the good, and the bad and right and the wrong. We have been men and we have been women.

I have to divert a little bit here because this is assuming something. It is assuming that everyone knows that they have been to this planet over and over again. Of course most people don't know that, the Christians don't because that part was taken out of the Bible after several reprints. Very few religions acknowledge rebirth.

Bodies die and bodies are reborn, but we are not born and we don't die. We are eternal, we are a consciousness. We adopt a body or a body adopts us so that we can be in this dimension. When the body dies, the consciousness remains. If it needs more experience, it finds another body.

We have developed this dimension in order to experience everything there is to experience about duality, to feel what it is like to be a man, to feel what it is like to be a woman. In order to do that, we had to forget who we were in our previous life, otherwise we would have carried these things through, gone on overload, and never really been a man, because we would remember being a woman and never really remember being a man because we could remember being a woman. We'd never really be with these new parents, because we could remember our past parents. Now, some children who are being born do remember their past lives, but that hasn't been appropriate for a long time. We have needed to think that each life is complete in itself. In fact, it is a complete section in itself, but the consciousness links all these.

We have experienced everything and in the process of that we have bent the laws. People talk about the original sin as if we are sinners, but that isn't true. It is not possible to break the law although it is possible to bend it. You can't break the law because the eternal law is what everything is built on. You can bend it, and that happens when you do something very unconscious, what we call evil or violent. These words are our words but don't really belong to the universe. When we do that, we bend the law, and to compensate for that we have to do or experience something so that balance can be achieved. We keep pushing things out of balance in our unconsciousness, and then rebalance is needed. In the East it is called karma but in the West we don't really acknowledge it. We just say, "Good will triumph in the end." But lifetime after lifetime it may not.

We have something called karma or imbalance. Through our lives we experience one thing and we need to also experience the opposite to balance it. It all has to do with experience, because that is expanding our own consciousness, and that of the universe. As we are all one and all connected, anything that any of us experiences affects everybody. That's why often, when you sleep badly or have an uncomfortable day, you find that people you work or live with have had a similar experience.

We are all linked, we are all connected, so every experience of one is the experience of many, whether it is realized or not. We created Planet Earth to go through the experiences of duality. To have sex, not to suppress it, to be in our emotions not to avoid them, to think our thoughts and not to stop them. If you do these things fully, they turn a cycle and then they are completed. When they are completed, they stop on their own. Planet Earth was designed for that and its work is done. We are asleep to that fact.

We have all these ridiculous ideas. Many people really believe that this is the only inhabited planet in the Universe, and when you look at how many billions and billions of planets there are in just this solar system, the chances of there being no other intelligent life are too minute to even consider. In fact, until comparatively recently, people thought that the earth was flat and the sun went round us.

Everything that the universe needs to get out of Planet Earth it has got, so it is going to be upgraded. Now I have to digress again.

I have been talking about Planet Earth as something separate, and that isn't true. The same way you have fingers and a nose and a liver and molecules that make up these parts, so we are making up Planet Earth. It is not a lump of rock, it is a living consciousness and we are part of it. Just as our livers are parts of our bodies, we are part of the planet. We don't like this very much because we like to be individuals. We are individuals in that we are unique and we have our own will, that is part of the law, but we are not separate and never can be, as we are part of Planet Earth and Planet Earth is part of us.

In our ignorance and greed and misunderstanding, and I don't say these words in any way judgmentally, we have raped the planet and are continuing to do so. The planet as a consciousness is saying, "Enough! You are going to kill me if you go on like this. I am not going to allow that so I am going to stop you." I want to express again that the planet is not separate from us. We are saying this on another level of our consciousness.

There is no time. Time is an illusion that belongs to this dimension. Some scientists have told us this and many people are starting to have glimpses of it, although they can't understand it. They can't because it can't be understood by the mind. Who you are going to be, you already are in another dimension, in another vibration. On this other level you, Roxi, have said that you need to stop destroying the planet. You have heard that in your consciousness so now you are careful about what you do and what you say and what you think. You have brought your consciousness to that. You are starting to be aware of not only your individuality, but your responsibility to the whole.

This is happening for more and more people now, but many others are still asleep, so they are being awoken by means that are not always pleasant. They get AIDS, cancer, heart diseases or one of these debilitating diseases, or they lose their money or they have a car crash or their beloved leaves them. The planet is shaking itself, and again the planet is not separate from us, so we are shaking ourselves from another dimension. We are shaking ourselves because we are saying that the experiment to experience duality is over. Planet Earth is going to change its vibrational level. What the Bible says is something like, "And the disciples will walk on earth." They are already walking on Planet Earth. All that is going to happen is our consciousness is going to be able to see them. They are going to be available practically to help people with the refinement of their consciousness. There is going to be peace on Planet Earth for 1000 years.

What has not been decided up to now is whether we are going to do this voluntarily or whether we are going to fight to the last.

If enough people start to wake up, especially people in power who have an effect on the planet, then it will be enough to cause a shift in consciousness. There will still be unpleasant times generally, but the transition will be comparatively smooth.

If there is a solid, contracted resistance to this change in consciousness, if people keep fighting the energy which is awakening in us, then something catastrophic may have to happen to earth. A pole shift has been foretold by some people. This would mean the planet would screech to a halt for a while, and then tilt over and start spinning in another direction. Earthquakes, plague, pestilence, all these things have been predicted by various people and something dramatic could happen if we don't voluntarily decide. But it may be something even more dramatic nobody has actually thought of yet, something totally unexpected. We may start to see different realities, so people start to see the entities that are around us, or start to disappear and reappear somewhere else. People may slip through time into the so called past and future. What is certain is that Planet Earth is not going to be allowed to continue as it is.

This experiment is over. It is up to us to accept this wonderful energy that's expanding within us and be prepared for changes on every level within and without. If we fight, then it will be unpleasant. If we go with them joyfully, we can enjoy the adventure and have a lot of fun.

CHAPTER TWO

CHILDHOOD

An Interview by Lady Chohan

Chohan: This is a series of interviews that we are going to be doing with you on the subject of the journey toward self–realization.

Paul: There isn't one, that's the trouble. The journey is because you think you need a journey. There is no journey.

Chohan: How about stages?

Paul: If you want stages, you can have stages. If you want a journey, you can have a journey. If you want to be there now, you can be there now. Whatever you decide.

Chohan: Can you talk about the stages that you have undergone in your...

Paul: I haven't undergone any stages. You see, this system has gone through stages, but I haven't. There is no continuity. Try again.

Chohan: I would like to talk to you about the subject of childhood. From what I know of your own childhood, you were a very unusual child. A little eccentric perhaps. The angle I would like to talk about childhood from is not just your own personal experience of being a child and what you were like as a child, but also childhood in general, what it means to be a child on Planet Earth. My first question to you is about you as a child. What do you remember, looking back? How much did you know of what was going to happen to you when you were a child?

Paul: I knew everything, but it wasn't in the memory bank that could deal with it. It wasn't supposed to be there. I knew everything, but I didn't know I knew. Everybody knows everything, now.

What I experienced was being in a very strange place. I didn't remember asking to be here. I saw a lot of odd things going on, and they somehow seemed to be strange in comparison to something, but I couldn't remember what the something was. Nothing really computed.

Nothing really made sense to me. People said one thing but did another. The very thing that they judged other people for was the thing that they usually did themselves. The way the transport was, what we lived in, it all seemed very weird. I used to think over and over again that these weren't my parents, that I'd come from somewhere else, but I didn't know there was a somewhere else.

I remember one of the first things I used to doodle at school was spaceships, before they were really talked about. I used to draw transport craft that were nothing like we'd ever dreamed about at that time. Something was coming through from somewhere, but I didn't know there was a somewhere for it to come through from. I remember life being very strange and not really wanting to live. It didn't seem worth it; it all seemed too painful.

When you are asking generally, I see a process like this. Being in the womb is not the pleasant experience most people assume it is. They see the child curled up and floating around and in an even temperature, being fed and so on. It's not such a pleasant process. I'm not saying that's so for the being, because maybe the being hasn't entered the foetus yet, but to the system it's not so enjoyable.

It's not so pleasant because every emotion, every thought, every distress that the mother goes through, the child is that. It's not separate. It is that system, so it's going through everything the mother is going through. If it's the first child, there is all the fear of the mother, the fear of the pain that's going to come. Every argument the parents have, every piece of insecurity, is all going through that system, so it's not so pleasant in there.

It's a very unpleasant process getting born. It's a shock coming out into bright lights and incredible noise and a great change of temperature. All of these things go on, but at that time the spirit isn't attached so it can watch all this. The system is going through it, but the being can watch.

Then slowly the spirit has to forget itself, so that it can integrate, otherwise the experiment won't work. What will happen is that the body will be born and start to grow, but the spirit will just stand off and watch it, because it doesn't want to get involved. Planet Earth is a very unpleasant experience. It has to forget and as it forgets, it becomes one with the body, but there is still some sort of remembering.

A child has no separation, it is just, "ising". If it's playing with a stone, there's no stone and there is no baby; there is just this phenomenon that includes everything. Whenever it does anything it's total, there's no separation. There is no thought and therefore there is no premeditation. That being is spontaneity. It isn't even spontaneous, it is just spontaneity. Whatever it does, it just does it, like a cat or a dog or a lion.

Then it starts doing things that don't get accepted, even right at the beginning. It starts crying in the middle of the night because it's wet or uncomfortable, or it's hungry or upset and it doesn't know where it is. It cries because it's uncomfortable and that's its instinctive way of getting attention, and thus getting things put right. The person that is to put this right, the mother or the father, is already on overload and has been since his or her childhood. They weren't coping with their own lives. They were normal and managing, but not coping. They had nothing to spare.

In fact, they probably had the child because their own lives were not working. If their lives had really been working, they wouldn't have needed to have the child. You don't need a child if every moment is a fulfillment in itself. There's no need to do anything. They had the child because life wasn't working and because that's what you do when you get married. Also the woman has her instinctive feeling. It's called the mothering instinct. It's just an animal feeling, that says that it's time to get pregnant and reproduce. It's a very basic energy.

So this being which is already on overload then takes on having a baby. She gives birth to it, and then has to hassle with the father, and probably with her parents, and his parents. All these problems are going on in her life and then the baby cries in the middle of the night. This being goes over there, trying as hard as possible to be loving and understanding and patient, but there is all this turmoil going on and inevitably she takes it over to the baby. Eventually the mother starts to say, "Shut up", or she just leaves it alone.

The baby then starts to compute things. When it's toddling around, it suddenly discovers a pot of honey that nobody had noticed, takes the honey, pours it onto the carpet making a wonderful mess. The honey, the jar, the carpet, are all part of the child's life. The mother or the father comes in, gets angry, and suddenly the baby starts to compute. It says, "Think before you do anything." Spontaneity has disappeared. The being has gone into retirement. The real life has gone. What it is avoiding is not right and wrong, whatever those things are, it is not to upset somebody else who has power over it. As a child, it needs to be taken care of and needs to survive. So it's got to be careful, do and say the right things, and not make trouble. Otherwise the love will be withdrawn and it will get thrown a lot of unpleasant energy. This is where the trouble begins.

Chohan: Two things come out of what you are saying. It seems that childhood is the place where everything goes wrong. It's as though one comes into this world as you describe, a vulnerable, innocent being and with a kind of a clarity and seeing. Then we learn to lie, we learn not to be who we are, we learn to cover that up. Something starts closing down. That process in childhood feels to me to be what we are trying to recover from when we are seeking to find our way back home. Is that right ?

The other question I have for you is, how did you survive your childhood, how did you survive this inevitable process?

Paul: Let's go back to the general thing first. A child is born in innocence. That's one level. It's also born with the effects of every previous life. So, everything that's happened to this entity, anything it's done, has to be balanced. If it's done beautiful things, then beautiful things will surround it. If it's done ugly things, ugly things will surround it. We're changing gear. You see, I have made out this child to be a victim.

This child is not a victim. That was one level of looking at it. Another level is that this child, before it manifested in this plane, chose to come here, because it needed to come here. On the other level it wasn't clearing what it needed to clear. It needed to come to a level that was material, where things could be done and experienced to balance the imbalance from previous lives. So it actually chose exactly the situation it was born into, because that's what it needed. If it had a parent that wasn't taking care of it, it needed that experience, possibly to balance a time when it didn't take care of its children in a previous life. A balance was needed. I say needed and that isn't true. Thus, we can move to a third level. In everything we talk about, there are levels and levels. It's which one are we going to look at, which one are we taking as our reality. Another level is this: that the child is born in innocence, because it never leaves innocence. We never leave innocence, it's always there. It has never not been there. It was never born and it will never die. Innocence just is. We stray from that in unconsciousness and we get further and further away. Nobody tells us that it is always available, that at any moment we can stop and go home, we can go to that place. We can just become quiet and still and reach, "The place of peace that passes all understanding." You can just go there. But we get further and further away, and that is part of the game. Until now.

There is now a new era on the planet where we don't have to go through all that. Now you can just wake up.

How did I survive? When you said that, I saw a scene of the junior school I went to. I was in class and I had a very bad earache. At first the teacher didn't believe me, but I must have really looked bad, so eventually he told me I could go home. It was in the afternoon and so I started walking. I think it was about three miles to where I lived. There was a lot of open countryside and this one deserted lodge. There was a path across a field and I was walking across this path. I must have been a little delirious because the earache was very bad. I then saw myself walking on another planet. Nobody had ever told me about planets. I knew nothing about them. It was like a desert. I was walking across this desert, but my feet weren't actually touching the ground. I remember feeling that I wasn't really there, so clearly that I felt I could leave this planet at any moment. Something in me wanted to leave and something else couldn't quite go.

Then I remember looking at everything in wonderment. I never took anything for granted. I still don't. The telephone is still a miracle to me. On one hand I can understand it, on the other picking it up and talking to somebody on the other side of the planet, as though they are in the next room, is still not taken for granted. I used to look at everything in that way.

In the school where I was, there were always gangs because it was a working class neighborhood. It was quite dangerous not to be in a gang, but I never was. Everything was strange. I used to spend a lot of time on my own. I used to go roller–skating for miles and miles along the streets. But the main thing my life was based on, from when I was about three or four years old, was singing. I had a very high, loud, clear voice. When I used to sing, I was gone. Now I know what gone is, but then I didn't understand what was happening. I just sang and I was gone. I was in the church choir, the school choir and the national choir. When I sang, I was oblivious to everyone and everything. In fact, I often used to get told that everybody had to follow me. I was usually the leader. The organist used to follow me because I had the loudest voice. I used to really live for that in a way, and being on my own and walking in the countryside.

Chohan: Is it not as though in some way as a child you found a dimension of the religious or the divine to connect into?

Paul: Without knowing it, the church was one of the most powerful places for me. When I used to sing, because of its shape and the echo, the sound used to take me away. Since that time, I've remembered moving energy that way on other planets in similar places.

Chohan: One thing I'd like to come back to is this idea of responsibility. In some way, traditional therapy is about undoing or letting go of childhood trauma. It seems to me that the only real way of unraveling our trauma is to have the perspective that we have created everything, that we created our parents and the situation that we were born into. In that way, there is a possibility of very quickly letting go of that conditioning. I wondered if you could say something more about that aspect or angle and also, looking back, why you think you created your parents? Why do you think you created this particular set of circumstances for yourself? What were you needing for your path?

Paul: I think my path is a bit different generally. My parents were part of our team and they volunteered to come here to take care of me, and to make sure I grew up with my maximum faculties available, although they don't remember this. My father came along as a vehicle and my mother came to take care of me. She did that in every way, in fact over took care of me. She felt she had this precious thing to take care of. That's why we got together, so that this system would grow up as uncontaminated as possible. They did pretty well. We didn't have television, magazines or books, and the radio was hardly ever on so, I was given as little conditioning as possible.

I only went to an elementary school and I left school at fourteen, so my system really was pretty uncontaminated. When you talk about this idea of responsibility, you are right. But, did *your* mother understand that? Does she understand that she was responsible for her parents and her situation? No.

When we are talking to people, we have to say it in such a way that they can start seeing this. You worked very hard, because even though you don't remember, on another level you remember who you are and what you came for. So your whole life has been about waking up. Many people are far away from that and that's fine because that's the way the planet was supposed to work. It was supposed to be that you were absolutely awake, then you forgot it all and afterwards worked your way through the stages because, as you did, you developed more experience.

But now that experiment is over. There is no time to work through the layers. We've had our time and now it's time to wake up. So we have to find out where we can start. Most people, of course, are not aware that they are responsible. They don't know where they come from. They don't know where they are going to. What we are talking about is just nonsense in their eyes. So we are looking at how we can get people started.

Therapy has tried, but the trouble is it is believing itself and therapy isn't true. It is just working on somebody who is unconscious, to try to help him to wake up. The trouble is usually that the therapists are unconscious too, because they believe their process. They haven't got to the place where they know that they are responsible for their lives. So, how do they do that? How does anybody do that? Well, I don't think anybody can unless circumstances produce something for them. Either you are born close enough to your consciousness and there is an inkling there, or you have a shock. Somebody close to you dies, or maybe you nearly die. Or you have some sort of spiritual experience, maybe through a drug or something just happens to you, and suddenly you know that there is something else. That's one of the values that LSD brought many people.

The intelligent people didn't continue with drugs. They saw that the drugs can't take them there, stopped taking them and said, "How can I find that for myself?"

Sometimes people get to this place through boredom. They become so successful, everything works for them so well, that they say, "Now what else is there?" They start reading through a few books or they meet somebody who has something different, and they want to investigate what else there is. If somebody is really asleep and they don't know they are asleep, what can you do?

The planet is going to do something. It's going to say, "Look, you are asleep and you haven't realized it. This is all an illusion but you don't know that, so we are going to start to show you. Life is going to be as though somebody has slipped LSD into your drink without you knowing it. Suddenly life is going to be different. You are going to see and experience things in a completely new way."

Then people are going to say, "Hey, something is happening. Who knows about this?" Then they will start looking. But if people are asleep and they don't know they are asleep, don't waste your time on them. Wait for the people who are starting to wake up and saying, "Do you have something to tell me?" These are the people to share with.

Chohan: I'd like to come back to the issue of childhood again. You have been a parent and you have two daughters. What would you say to a parent at this particular time, this unique time that we are living in?

Paul: Well, if you are not a parent, my advice would be don't become one, there isn't time, there isn't the energy. You need your energy to find out who you are. If you are a parent already, what can you do?

Chohan: I have a feeling that you have some advice on how to treat children as human beings, how to recognize the potential in every child who is growing in this new age. I'm thinking of your own daughter Ryan, and how extraordinary she is. I know she's been through as much trauma as any child has, and at the same time she seems to be a very special human being. It does seem that the children that have been born at this time are special.

Paul: A lot of them are, but not all. Remind me of that and I'll come back to children who are being born now. Bringing up a child is impossible. A child needs total attention. Total. When it comes out of the womb, it's only just started its waking up process. It needs all our attention. We don't have the time, we can't even give ourselves total attention. We don't accept ourselves. How can we accept anything else? Even with all the right intentions, we don't know how to do it.

But in theory, this is what you do: In Africa, in many of the tribes, the mother always carries the child. Now some carry them on the back, some carry them on the side, and some carry them on the front. The ones that are carried on the front are less neurotic than the ones who are carried on the side. The ones carried on the side are less neurotic than the ones carried on the back.

When I say they are carried on the front, I mean they are always carried on the front. Always. If the mother really has to do something else, she hands the child to its grandmother. The child always has body contact and a breast there whenever it wants to feed. There are no restrictions whatsoever. It pees when it wants, it shits when it wants, it does everything it wants. It is totally accepted. These kids don't cry. When they start running around, they laugh and laugh and laugh. They have a very hard life by our standards, but they are only laughter, especially the ones carried on the front. The only time they are put down is when they start to want to go down. Then they are watched, but never stopped, they are allowed to do what they want. So if they hurt themselves or they bump them-

selves, they learn for themselves. They are not told anything, so everything gets integrated.

What develops is not a very sophisticated being but a
very sensitive one, a child who can smell animals miles and
miles away, who can hear things that we've never heard,
who can see things we've never seen. They can look at a
spore or a track, and just by looking at it, they know exactly when the animal went by. All sorts of things get
developed, but nothing gets in the way.

It's difficult, but that's what the child needs. Say the
child gets a pen in its hand and it has watched you draw
something, so it wants to draw. Of course, it hasn't computed that you did it on a piece of paper. It sees a big blank
area on the wall so it does it there. The child doesn't want
restrictions. We've got restrictions and mostly we restrict
them to death. They need space, they need to be able to
do what they need to do, as an experiment.

They love learning for themselves. At best, every thing
you tell them blocks off a learning experience. At worst,
you tell them a lie because you learned a lie, and you just
pass the lie on. You don't know it, you never experienced
it for yourself. You just took what somebody else told you
for granted. It's not your truth.

We are constantly conditioning the child with lies.
What we think is the truth is usually what someone told us
is the truth. It's not our truth because we haven't found out
for ourselves. It isn't ours. So the advice is, leave the child
alone as much as you possibly can. Of course you don't
want them messing up the whole house, so give them a
room which is theirs, where they can go totally wild.

Now, there are a few little things to watch. One is not
to let them hurt themselves. But then you have to be very,
very aware. If they are walking on a wall where there is a

big drop, and they could really hurt themselves, somehow get them to see that for themselves. Don't just take them off, let them see it. If it's a minor danger, let them do it, let them find out. If they are playing with candles, let them play with candles. Be there, watch. Let them put their fingers in for themselves and then they will know. You don't have to tell them anything. It's gone into their systems and it's their experience. If they ask you what God is or where you come from, you can say, "This is what I've heard, this is where I've got to so far on this subject. This is what I think. Find out for yourself."

Chohan: I remember hearing a very well known psychotherapist say to an audience that children don't need perfect parents. Last night, Clare, who is the mother of your daughters, said that she realized that she and Ryan had reached a stage in their relationship where they had forgiven each other for being mother and daughter.

Paul: We're changing gear again, and we're talking about the child choosing its parents because it needed to go through that. Earlier, you said special children are getting born now. They are being born, but they are being born to looser people because these people are more likely to allow them to be who they are.

But you see, Ryan didn't need to go through all that. She needed to go through that only because she thought she needed to go through it. Nobody needs to go through anything anymore. It is possible to wake up now. If we keep letting go of our ideas, it just makes everything so much easier and smoother. There are a lot of extraordinary beings being born now. A lot of them are coming here because this is the high spot of the universe at the moment, this is the most exciting place. You have astronovas and you have stars that burst and are very dramatic, but here there is an explosion of consciousness. This planet is about to burst out from the primitive into the exalted. This is a very exciting time. Some entities have come and are watching, but you can't see them. Others say, "I really want to experience this. I'm going to take a body at this time." So they look around for people who have prepared themselves a bit and then they get attracted to each other. They get as little impediment as possible in their growth. Then many other people, some in bodies and some out of bodies, are here just to help at this time. Some of them have said, "Well, you can only do so much when you channel or when you are around as an influence. If you really want to help the planet, you have to get into one of these things. Then you start to have experiences that are more easily communicable."

In one way, you can be more effective in a body, and in a strange way you can't. People will go to somebody who's channeling and give much more credence to the channeling. They'll say, "This is magic. This is coming from somewhere else. This must be true." But they are less likely to act on it than somebody who has that consciousness in himself or herself.

CHAPTER THREE

SEXUALITY

An Interview by Lady Chohan

Chohan: You are perhaps the one person in the world that I know who has explored their sexuality totally. You have gone into areas that most people would probably be afraid to go into, areas that they do not even think about going into. It seems that at this stage in your life you have come through. Could you say something about this process of totality with sexuality and what it's like to come through?

Paul: What is most interesting about what you have just said is, come through. You are seeing it in a certain way and most people don't see it that way. Most people don't want to come through, because if they come through sex, there isn't much to live for. They don't know that, but somewhere either having sex or not having sex gives them a reason to live. For them, once sex is over, either doing it or not doing it, going with it or suppressing it, then there is no reason to live. In a way that's true. When you stop reproducing, you are not useful anymore in animal terms.

I would see that as the basis of most of the distress on this planet.

Most violence is based in sex. It has to do with sexual suppression, which is still being practiced on the planet on every level. Whether there is promiscuity or whether there is suppression, it's still the same thing. It has to do with sex not being natural. How exactly it got this way, I have no idea. I'm not a historian. But it looks like we weren't allowed to be ourselves. Somebody got a little bit embarrassed about it, somewhere. Or maybe somebody decided if they suppress sex, they can then control people through that, because people feel guilty. You can't suppress sex. You can suppress its actions, but you can't suppress its thoughts.

Sex is a fact. We are born with it. Man is supposed to be born with more than women, but that's not true, we are all born with the same. It just looks more obvious in one way and less obvious in another. It's an absolute power. Women probably experience this in a slightly different way than men do.

At a certain age in a male, when he is a boy, this energy arises. There is nothing he can do about it. It rises in such a way that it colors everything. It doesn't matter what you look at or what you think about. It's in your dreams, it's in your thoughts during the day. Whatever you are looking at, sex is there. There is this energy that says, "Fuck." It doesn't say make love and it doesn't say get married. It just says, "Do it," just like a horse or a rabbit does. It's just an animal energy and we try to suppress it. I suppose, if we were intelligent about it, and had some enlightened teaching that said, "How can we be with this energy?" then maybe we could take it into different channels and that this could be useful. But we are made to feel guilty with it and then it becomes a suppression. It's that energy, that was suppressed, that didn't flow, that turns into cancer or a heart attack or some disease that kills us. It can be argued that that isn't so, "I know so and so and they have done it all their life and..." They didn't do it all their life. They did the action but they never gave themselves total permission. If people give themselves total permission with that energy, they will not be violent, they will not be angry, they will not be hurting. That energy will just flow through them and it will become God. That is what it is.

It's our suppression of that energy that is probably the source of most of the trouble on the planet.

Chohan: Could you say something about your own experiences from the time when you were an adolescent to the present day? That's quite a large topic, I guess! How did you learn to use this energy? How did you give yourself total permission?

Paul: I remember this energy rising and not really knowing what it was because nobody talked about it. There were drawings in the toilets at school, but I couldn't even understand the women's side. I didn't know anything about anything, and nobody was telling me, nobody talked about it. I remember my mother saying, "You can ask me anything." One time I asked her one small question and she hit me so hard I fell in the bath. So that was the end of that subject! It was just because she was so embarrassed, she wasn't at ease with it. There was no sex education at school, people just told dirty stories. This energy in me grew and somewhere I picked up the idea that it was not a good thing, you were not supposed to have this.

In fact, one very cute thing happened. At one stage my father very embarrassingly gave me a book that looked as though it had come from some ancient library. It was falling apart and all the pages were yellow. It must have been handed down for generations. In that book, it actually said that you will go blind if you masturbate. As I was masturbating every day at that time, I was thinking about making myself a white stick! So this energy was boiling there and I wasn't supposed to do anything with it. It was wrong and bad, it did this and did that.

The energy wasn't allowed to move, so one thing I did was take up cycling. I used to cycle 1000 miles a month in my spare time, fast, until I would literally drop. I would burn it up however I could. I didn't get married until I was twenty three and I hadn't had sex until then. Then I found out that the woman I had married didn't like sex so much, so this energy just burned and burned. I was very embarrassed and very shy and so full of energy. I didn't want to upset women, or even show it, because I believed that women didn't want sex, and it was a drag for them. I felt like I was imposing something, so I avoided them. The energy stayed so strong that I started to suppress it and to hold it back in every way I could. I did that for years. It was just a burning force inside.

Then one day I came to the conclusion that I couldn't hold it anymore. I literally thought I was going crazy. I could feel the energy sneaking off into other places and unbalancing everything. So, I said to myself, "I've got to do it." How I got to this place of giving myself permission, I don't know. So every woman I was attracted to I asked if she wanted to go to bed with me. At times I was excruciatingly embarrassed and I often couldn't ask, I was shaking so much. Then to my surprise, a lot of women started to answer yes and so I started doing it and doing it and doing it. It looked like it was never going to end. What I didn't like about the suppressed feelings was I couldn't see a woman as a being. She was someone to release this energy. There was always love and there was always caring but there was also this energy which was stronger than both of us.

A lot of beautiful things happened through that, but there was always something there that wasn't beautiful. It was as if I had to do it, and if I didn't, I was suppressing and holding, and that would make things ugly. It looked like it was never going to end. By this time, I'd started to realize that I'd come to this planet for something else, but this was consuming my whole life in some way. At some point I remember thinking that it looks like I'm not going to be able to do anything but deal with this energy. I then decided that I was going to do as much as I possibly could with it.

With that decision, something started to change. It felt as if I wasn't going through it anymore, I was going into it. I didn't know whether there was a way through it, so I went into it for the sake of going into it, rather then going through it. Then something changed. It changed its rhythm, its path. It became slower, it became more beautiful, less driving. I had periods where it disappeared and there was no drive at all.

I remember that being a very beautiful part of my life and in one way there was a sort of sadness when it went. It had become fun, because I had a choice in it. Then in another way, I could now meet a woman as a being, I didn't need anything anymore. I could just see her for who she was without needing anything or having to do anything.

Then that would disappear and the energy would come back again. By that time I had learned just to say yes and to be available to that energy. It became softer and softer and more and more loving, more and more caring and less and less physical, until it just started to dissolve. The energy got incorporated in another way. I found that I was more loving and that I really loved people. It felt like when the passion was there the love couldn't be there, so there was always a tension.

Then, as that dissolved, something else happened. This may be a little bit discouraging for people who are on the other side of it. I felt as though I was in a spacesuit. There was a me, and there was a something that watched the spacesuit. It's like, when I hold someone's hands, two spacesuits are holding hands, not two beings, not two people. There is something beautiful about the touching, but it is also so gross and so crude, it's like material touching. While we are invested in this it takes away from that infinite space that is inside. We are two nothings becoming one nothing. I see that's the basis for all religion. The taboo against sex is true, but it's been perverted and distorted. While one is still addicted to sex, and I'm not saying it's something one does, I'm saying it's a natural addiction, then energy isn't available for something else. Then what most people do is, because of the connotations around it, because of the guilt around it, because of the holy teaching around it, they keep trying to get over it.

What I suggest is, don't get over it, go into it, get lost in it, be so total that something else can happen. When that happens, you come out into another place. You don't go into it to go through it, because that still means you have some judgment about it.

Chohan: As you are telling your story, there is something very poignant that I'm feeling. It's the sense of this beautiful being trapped, or having to be a slave to an energy that's not natural. And yet, as you surrender to this energy, I can feel that you are finding your own way home through it. Surrendering to this energy is taking you home. That feels as though that has been a primary part of your process.

Paul: My process at the moment is that I don't even know if there is a home. That's still an idea and maybe you have had glimpses of it and home means something to you. I did have glimpses and home did mean something to me, but it doesn't mean anything now. I don't know what home is anymore. As you were talking, what I saw was that this energy was absolutely natural to this machine. It's not natural to the higher state of vibration, but it has to be included. If we have decided to come here to this planet and manifest in this form, we cannot go around this energy. Now, some people might have been born with such a high vibration that it won't be a problem, but it still has to be included. Nothing can be excluded. Whatever level of vibration and consciousness is reached, it includes everything. It's just that when the main vibration reaches a higher level, this is transformed; but it still exists. I have that with you. I love you and I could say I'm attracted to you. But it's not sexual and it's not physical. It's your glory and your beauty, of which you are not aware most of the time.

It is just very beautiful and wonderful. This wants to be there, but it can't do the sexual thing anymore because it is irrelevant. The sexual thing goes away from this beauty. That sort of feeling is totally opposite to the other thing that wants to happen, which is it just wants to dissolve.

There was a point of great distress, and I have had this with you, when this attraction would be there and I would want to be with you, but then when we got together, I didn't know what to do, because something of the animal was still there. Something was still there with sex and it wanted to be with you sexually. But then, when it was, it was totally inappropriate. It didn't know what to do. It was a transition stage and this is very uncomfortable, because it's got a foot on both sides with neither of them complete and neither of them working. Again, you've got to be there. And, what I have said over and over is, from my experiences, if there is any doubt whether you need to be with somebody or not, be with them. Don't use the mind to avoid anything, just have the courage to follow it, even when it's fading. If you do, it will transform and if you don't, it will not. You may suppress it, you may hold it down, you may tuck it away, but it will come back. It will come back in your dreams. It will come back when you reach a stage when your energy force is not strong enough to hold it down.

That's what happens with a lot of people when they get old. They suppressed and suppressed and in some way sex has become irrelevant to them, but only because they held it. Then they get old and they don't have that energy anymore, but it starts to arise and it's totally inappropriate, because the body isn't suitable for it. So then they are in the very uncomfortable position of having a sexual energy that they are not capable of fulfilling and it can turn into a disease. You cannot suppress sex and you cannot hold that energy. It will always come back up again.

Chohan: Two questions arise about following that energy wherever it's triggered. The first question I have is about relationships. How to find the balance between, on the one hand what people call promiscuity, and on the other hiding your sexuality and playing safe in a relationship. Where do we find that balance between exploring our sexuality and intimacy? What is the connection there?

Paul: The second most destructive thing on this planet is relationships. They are killing this planet, because the relationships are of the mind, not of the energy. There may be a natural cycle within us, of about four years, to be with somebody. That's to do with having children. Be with somebody until the child is about four years old and then the mother can take care of it herself. We are not honest. If any of you look back to your relationships, you'll find you never left when it was over. You hung on and dragged it down, sometimes for years. Sometimes people have been married for fifty years and the relationship was really over in the second year. They didn't have the courage to leave. We don't have the courage to be honest with ourselves and admit a relationship is over.

There are stages of relationship, and if you follow them, you'll evolve. If you don't, you won't evolve. The first relationship is in the teens when the energy is very volatile and it doesn't matter whom it's with. It has this crush on this person, forever, and it can last three or four days, maybe three or four weeks. It's totally consuming and then it's over. It was never meant to be anything else. All it was meant to be was just an experiment, a release of energy. Find out about each other and then move on and move on.

Then, if we listen again, we'll find that that's not quite so relevant. We need to be with somebody for a longer time and live with them, but not forever and not for marriage and all that nonsense. It is coming together and discovering what a man is and what a woman is and what it's like to live together, being in some close space and seeing what it is like to cohabit, then letting it go. You need to be in wrong relationships, so you can learn with whom you are compatible, to learn what's useful and what isn't useful. You need to experiment and then you let that go. Then another relationship comes along that's a different level, where you come together in a deeper way, but you still need to be with other people as well. You need to do that because everybody has to pass through jealousy. Everybody has to experience it on every level. They need to know the ugliness of it. And then you let that go.

Keep moving through the stages of relationship, never holding, just being ruthlessly honest, acknowledging when it's finished and letting it go. If you keep doing that, you come to a place where you don't need a relationship, because you have become so complete and so total in yourself. You are not looking for anybody to lean on or anybody to fill the part where you are not complete in yourself. You have become whole. At that point, if you meet somebody who is also in that state, then something very beautiful happens. Most relationships are ninety percent ugly, either because they are fighting, or because they are holding back and not expressing their truth to each other. Most people just don't have the courage to be themselves in relationships.

Chohan: The question that just flashed into my mind was: "What would happen if people really did express their truth in relationships?"

Paul: Wonderful chaos, to start with. All the lies would be cut and blown. People would be freaking out and throwing dishes and breaking windows; just releasing themselves. It would be good if somebody was around to say, "Look what's happening. Look at your process. Look, your whole world is falling apart, because the control has been lifted. Now let's find out who we really are."

So, you go to a party and your boss is a woman, and she brings her husband with her who is very handsome. You are not going to even allow yourself to think about being attracted to this man because of your boss. If you do show anything, she is almost certainly going to make trouble for you. You suppress your feelings and your truth and that's what eventually kills you, that's what gives you diseases. If you didn't do that, you would go up to the husband and say, "I'm attracted to you." Then there would be something going on with your boss and with your husband. The truth could come out.

When you walk into a room where a party is happening, it's lies, layer and layer and layer of lies. All those lies are poison. They poison the person, they poison everything around, they poison the planet. In a way that it is hard to understand, they are poisoning the sea, the air, the trees. It's our lies that are poisoning everything. We blame pollution or the hole in the ozone but they're not, it's our lies. If we didn't lie, we wouldn't pollute anything, we would live in truth. If we went into that room in truth there would be an explosion of white light. We would all come down in pieces, but we would come down in truth. We would come down in light and then we could start to question everything.

We don't do that because there is a system here that is so powerful, that just wants to survive.

How do you survive? Well, a woman survives if she has got a man to protect. How does a man survive? He survives if he has got a woman to take care of, and so on. We are all surviving. It's not needed, we'll all survive if we let go. We'll not only survive, we'll live in light, but it takes great courage. If you start doing that, your life will totally change and there will be a level of chaos around you, but you will start to emerge into the light.

Chohan: The world would be a very, very different place, if we all started living on that level.

Paul: Well, you have experienced it here. That's how we started out the Six Month Project. One relationship after another, one lie after another, locked into each other. It looks like love, but often it was basically lies. Sex confused everything, too. We said, "Stop holding on to everything, tell the truth." The truth came out, "I don't like you for doing this. I don't like you for doing that. I'm attracted to this." The whole thing disappeared and then there was just chaos. Now what's happened is most of the relationships have come back together, but in a totally different way. The ones that were real came back together, but they came back in truth and light. The ones that were false disappeared. Something very beautiful happened through people being encouraged and supported in letting go of their lives.

Chohan: Another question I have about sex has to do with what we call "tantra." There are many different traditions which come under that title and I am wondering how you feel about it? How do you see the function of what people call tantra which usually means the transformation of sexual energy?

Paul: All the tantric schools I have ever met are utter bullshit. They are just a way of having an idea of what you can do with sex and then controlling it. In one way it is damaging. It's going nowhere with that energy. You have to say yes to that energy first. I don't know the facts, but my guess is that tantric schools went through years of training before they came to this place that people are now trying to use as techniques. The techniques are just a form of suppression.

The sexual energy is an incredibly powerful energy and so if it can be gently channelled into other directions, that can be used for transformation. But it takes a master or a mistress, and years of training, to do that. Here, it has happened for many people after six months with no training, no techniques and no guidance. All that was suggested was, "When in doubt do it, and just keep doing it." If you do that, the animal channel gets satisfied and it thinks it has done its job and everything settles down. Tantra is happening for many people here, but it's not called tantra, and they don't even know it's tantra.

What happens is this. When the energy is aroused and needs to move, instead of going up into the animal state, it doesn't need to do that. So it just stays there and it stays very soft and very loving. The animal state builds a tension, it builds and builds and explodes in some way and that has to do with conception. This other doesn't do that. It stays gentle and leads to an orgasm, but not through tension. It moves up a totally different set of channels. It moves up very softly and gently and then it continues. There is no climax to it because it is a continual climax. It does that naturally so it is very beautiful. Many people then find that to have an orgasm is a downer, it just blows something away and wastes it.

Whereas if they stay with this very softly, it is like a continual orgasm and a continual energizer. Then they can come away in that state or go to sleep in that state and it doesn't have to be discharged. That's tantra; it's taking the energy up into these different channels so that it just gently opens chakras on the way.

Chohan: What you are describing is so different from the kind of sexuality that is usually written about in women's magazines, where there is much more emphasis on the quest for an orgasm, and on having certain kinds of physical pleasure. It feels to me that what we are discovering here is something very different. It's not dramatic, yet there is a level of subtlety and exquisiteness that isn't present in the other kinds of sex. What I feel you talking about has very much to do with the path of awareness, the path of relaxation, the path of sensitivity. I wonder if everybody is interested in that?

Paul: If you have decided to be in the percussion section in an orchestra, before you play the triangle, you need to try the timpani. You need to really bash those drums and let that energy out, because if you take all that energy to a triangle, you are going to be very frustrated. So this is part of what's needed. You need to be an animal, especially women, because men have somehow had much more permission to do it, and women never really have. Not only have they never had permission, but if they do go for it, the man usually gets scared and runs away. You need to have that permission to be that animal energy, to be really wild, to let go. They need to find a partner who is brave enough to be in that situation so they can let that energy go.

They need to move and make their noises and have their orgasms and just let what wants to happen happen. Once that has happened something changes in a woman. You can tell when a woman has had a great orgasm the following morning. She just glows, because all those channels are complete. They have had the exercise they need. If you try going into tantra before this has happened, it's all totally twisted. You need to experience it.

For the sake of some of the people who may be reading this, this isn't so with all women. Some women are born in a much higher state of vibration and they never need to have an orgasm, but these are very few. These are very special people who have come down to this planet just to help. Most women need to express that wonderful and awful energy, that animal that comes through that just wants to fuck with no mind. Doesn't care what is the other side of that, doesn't care about the name of the man or who he is. Once that has had its permission, then it becomes more subtle and more gentle, providing you keep having the courage to stay with suitable partners. A woman might be with a man who can provide that energy, who is that rough, but then he doesn't want to move on when she is ready. He wants to stay there, he doesn't want to grow. She then has to leave because otherwise she will get stuck at that level.

When you are talking about magazines and the advice they give, the trouble is that they are dealing with sex as a symptom and not as a source. They are trying to make it work. You can't make it work. It's not supposed to work. It's something that's transitory if you go into it totally.

Chohan: The question that naturally arises when talking about sex, and experimenting with many different partners, is the fact that we have AIDS on the planet. In some way, AIDS feels like a message or a teacher to me. I feel there is something that we have to learn from it. There must be a way that we can transform, that we can express our sexuality without suppressing it, with more awareness. Perhaps there are ways of letting go into sex that we haven't discovered yet.

Paul: As I was saying, when you reach a certain stage, sex is an embarrassment. It is so crude, it is so, I was going to say, inhuman, but the trouble is it is so human. It's so animal. The way to get to the stage you are talking about is by letting go inside and reaching a level of purity.

AIDS is an attitude, it's not a disease. It's what we call a disease, but we have produced it through an attitude. We've produced it through our guilt. We've produced it through our not wanting to live, because we can't handle this planet as it is. I have absolutely no medical knowledge whatsoever, but my feeling is that everybody has AIDS, whatever AIDS is. It is either activated or not activated. It's like having a cold or having herpes, it's just dormant or active and what makes it active is an attitude. Then we said it's happening in certain places. Generally we now have a different level of pressure of energy on the planet, and it's exploding the things that we have been holding.

Now, I know many people, and it's also happened to me, that have been in direct situations of contact with people who have had venereal disease. They have found out afterwards that the person had the disease, but they did not catch it. I have never had a venereal disease and I know many other people who also haven't, despite being in contact with people who have.

On the other hand, I also know people who have diseases all the time. We could say it has to do with resistances in the body, that the body is a reflection of our attitudes. I absolutely advise everybody to take every possible precaution with AIDS, and that means not only using condoms, but using condoms that are recommended for this particular use, as some condoms evidently let AIDS though. You have got to make sure and take every possible precaution because AIDS is much bigger than we realize, much, much bigger. The explosion is yet to happen.

But it's better to die of AIDS and die consciously than suppress, because then you will die unconsciously and you will come back again and again until you get it. Take every possible precaution, be careful, but that energy has to move.

If you are ready to let go totally, then no sex is needed, nothing is needed. You are there, you are in this expansion. It is possible to meditate and do it, but then it isn't just letting go in sex. You've got to let go of your partner, you have to let go of your work, your money, your possessions. I am not saying you've got to get rid of them, you have to let go of everything and say, "What is appropriate for me? Where am I to be, what are my needs?" And you are not asking anybody else, you are just asking your higher Self, you are asking that place in you that knows.

It's possible not to go through any stages. They are an attitude, all stages are an idea, are conditions. It is possible to just pop through. And that is what is going to happen. As some people reach their luminosity, others are going to see that, and they are going to say, "But it took you this and this and this and it took you years." The being is going to reply, "But now I know you don't need to do the same. Listen to me, you don't need to. It can happen now." And this energy is going to be so strong and so true and so real, people are just going to reach that place and pop through themselves.

Chohan: So the perspective or the direction that I am seeing now isn't necessarily focusing on sex. The important thing seems to be finding a space in which we learn to recognize our holding, whatever form it takes, and letting go of it. It feels to me that whatever I have discovered in this process we have been experimenting with has very much to do with recognizing the holding and letting it go. It seems as though it is as simple as that.

Paul: If the let go is total, then it can be that you might still be in the early stages of sex and you meet someone who is very attractive to you. Your whole system goes through all the things that it goes through when it gets that attracted and you are on fire with it. You are ready to go where you need to go, even if it means propositioning your boss's husband, while your husband is standing there. You're ready to follow this energy, risk of AIDS or anything. You say yes, but you don't do anything. You just say yes to that energy totally, with total awareness with total availability and it will move to another level, then another level and then another level. And in that moment, in no time at all, you are free.

Chohan: That feels like a very wonderful possibility and at the same time it seems people would need to be educated in what awareness is. When you talk about awareness, what do you mean?

Paul: They are going to be educated in awareness because the world is going to get into such a mess that people are going to need a new education. They are going to be aware that they need education, and then all the people who are training themselves at the moment, like people here who have spent six months of day and night total devotion to this process, are going to be available. After the six months, they are going to continue with their process, bringing that awareness into the world. Then these people are going to train other people and they in turn will train others, and when the time comes when the planet needs help, popping up all over the planet will be people who will be available.

All they will do will be to offer a little guidance and a little help and encouragement. Then people can do it themselves. Everyone has the possibility within him or her of tuning into other entities and other levels. They can tune into their guides and inner Selves and have all their questions brought into their own plane. There are many, many people, in and out of bodies, just waiting for that time when the planet says, "Yes, I now want to know."

CHAPTER FOUR

RELATIONSHIPS

An Interview by Lady Chohan

Chohan: What do you see as the function of relationships?

Paul: Learning not to do it.

Chohan: Would you like to elaborate on this?

Paul: Most relationships are to fill in the empty space within ourselves because we don't feel complete. We're not enough unto ourselves so we look for somebody else to fill in that space and then we don't have to look at the place that's incomplete within ourselves. The other person is doing the same, so both are trying to take from and lean on each other, and because it doesn't work there's resentment. If it does work for a while there's fear that the other will go away. Resentment then comes and the power of that person is given away to the other.

Underlying every relationship there is fear, anger and jealousy. All these things are cooking away because this person is relying on the other to make him or her complete.

Chohan: It seems to me that relationships are one of the most powerful learning experiences in terms of seeing who you really are, of seeing aspects of yourself mirrored in the other person that need to be seen and accepted and resolved: this can be to experience jealousy or to experience the ability to resolve conflict, or to learn to love somebody.

Paul: It is a learning process, but most of us don't go into it as that, and that's why it doesn't work. If it's gone into as a learning process, then it is more rapid than being on your own. If it were left alone, the natural course of a relationship would go like this.

As the sexual energy starts to rise, then a young person wants to play with the opposite sex. It plays and it becomes sexual which leads to intercourse. It then becomes very intense for a few days then breaks up. If it were left alone, that's what would happen. The sexual energy would follow a natural flow, an animal flow. It's very powerful, it's very intense. It's discharged and there's this cycle. If it's completely left alone with no taboos around it whatsoever, the energy then starts to flow out and wants to spend more time with one person, but still not to stay with them. This system is still looking for the right person to be with because it's a biological system for reproduction. If that's allowed, then some experimental relationships happen and then they fall apart, and then a deeper one begins. Then there are relationships where the people are together, but they still go on experimenting with others. Each one goes through their jealousy and their upsets about this, and eventually, through relating, maturity can happen more quickly. But the maturity only happens when you realize you are alone.

You are ultimately alone. When that is realized you stop looking outside of yourself. Then a peace comes. You may not be complete in yourself but you realize you're not going to find it out there. It's in here. You start looking for it inside and then a maturity starts to deepen. If during this time you meet someone else who has realized they're alone, that it can't be attained on the outside and they're looking for it on the inside, you can share a life together very beautifully. There will never be any possession because both people will realize you can't possess another.

When you say it's a learning process, that is true. If a person isn't in a relationship, what happens is they spend a short time with somebody and then when they get annoyed or displeased with this person, they say, "This person is unpleasant, I'll leave them." So they leave and they keep going away without realizing that whatever is going on in that person is a reflection of themselves. If they stay in a relationship they get themselves mirrored. This assumes a certain level of awareness which most people don't have. In practically all societies, the conditioning is such that you do this over and over again. The theory is that you find someone, you spend some time together, get married, have children and live happily ever after. It's still there even though everybody knows it doesn't work. There's always this hope that it's going to be on the outside. If it isn't the relationship, it'll be money, success, or fame and none of these things works. A relationship is a quicker way of finding this out.

Chohan: What I'm thinking about now is that in a general sense in the world, people are finding that relationships don't work, that marriage doesn't work, that contracts don't work. There's a higher divorce rate than there's ever been. At the same time, for those who are searching, there's often an obsession for what's called a soul mate, which seems to be what you're describing. That's someone with whom it would be possible to share this journey to awakening as an equal partner. Is there anything you have to say about the idea of soul mates?

Paul: It's usually an escape. Again, a person wants to find someone on the outside who's going to make life easier. I'm not saying there aren't soul mates, because that is not true. There are many soul mates and they can be the same sex or the opposite. They are people whom you've been with many times in different lives, people who closely mirror your opposite, and others who mirror the same, and with whom you feel a connection.

It is possible to meet a soul mate, that is somebody who resonates on the right level of energy to stimulate your own energy so you can look at yourself more clearly, experience yourself more clearly. But the trouble is that most people don't see it as that. They want that to do it and that can't do it. If you find someone within that right vibration, it can stimulate your vibration, but it has to be within the Self. So when people say to me, "Is it possible to have a soul mate?" what they are usually saying is, "Please, let be there something so I don't have to face myself on my own."

Chohan: When you are ready to give up that seeking to complete yourself on the outside, and you don't desire a relationship or want it in that way, is something possible then?

Paul: The very question is saying that you want that to happen. If you want that to happen, it cannot. If there's any wanting, if there's any desire, if you haven't given up relationships, then it's impossible for them to work. If you're still saying, "If I give them up will I still find somebody?" then you haven't given them up. It has to be, "I'm really ready to be on my own and work on my own." Then that is possible, but at that point you're choiceless about it.

Chohan: Can you say or describe what that's like, to be with somebody in that way?

Paul: It's like being on your own. It's just a harmony where everything dances together and nothing ever clashes. Everything just flows and moves beautifully and you enjoy each other just because you enjoy each other, not because you need anything, not because you want anything. There are no expectations. There's no wanting. If something arises, you may present that, but there's no expectation, there's no judgment, so it just becomes a floating.

You were saying, "Can relationships be learning processes?" They are, but the trouble is they're unlearning the main thing we need to learn. What we need to learn is we are not separate, there is only the One. Everything is connected, every one of us is connected. People think they can learn that in a relationship, but they can't. What you learn is another form of separation and it is one of the most destructive things. That is what I was talking about earlier, the cycles of relationship. The cycle that most people get stuck in is trying to be monogamous, trying to say, "This is the person who's going to supply everything I need and there's nothing else." People desperately want to do that because it makes a lot of trouble if you don't. It makes trouble because it disturbs your own system when you're moving around, and it certainly disturbs your partner and they're almost definitely going to make a lot of trouble for you. So every person is trying to make this work, and it doesn't.

It doesn't for this reason: if we go back to the animal level, the instinct in a woman is to capture a man. It's always a man is supposed to capture a woman but that isn't true. There's a line in a song that goes something like, "A man chases a woman until she catches him." The woman needs to capture a man biologically because she needs to get pregnant and then be taken care of. That's the biological process. The man's energy doesn't work like that. His basic energy is that of a hunter. It goes out and moves. That's one of the fundamental differences.

What happens is the woman tries to hold the man instinctively and somewhere he wants to be held, because when he's held, he's getting taken care of. Then up comes this energy. It is also not widely recognized, but after a woman has a child and she has reached a certain stage, her energy moves out too. The reason she doesn't follow it as much as men do is only social conditioning.

So a couple get together and they lock into each other to the exclusion of the rest of the five billion people on the planet, and that is against letting go of duality. We're here to realize duality and let it go.

If I'm in a fixed relationship and I meet you at a party, I'm not available to you and you're not available to me. I have a program that only allows me to see certain parts of you. If I start to acknowledge that I'm attracted to you, I'm going to go through all sorts of things inside. If I'm attracted to you and I start to follow that attraction, then I'm going to want to spend time with you, then I'm probably going to want to make love with you. After that, I may not want to be with my existing partner. Maybe she's pregnant, or she's just had a child, or we have just set up a house, or maybe she'll find out and throw pots and pans at me, so I don't see you and I don't open to you. You're probably going through the same sort of thing so we don't meet. We don't meet the person in the street, we don't meet the person behind the counter when we're buying something in a shop. We don't meet because we have got all these consequences that are going to complicate our lives. When somebody has become really free, they have moved wherever they want to go.

When you're in a relationship, you're usually suppressing the man and the woman. Traditionally, it's the man that goes out and sows his oats, but it's only social conditioning that holds back this same energy in a woman. A woman wants to move and we don't allow that. We didn't allow that when we were in our teens, so we have locked up sexual energy. When we first meet somebody and start a relationship, we usually have a lot of sex. As soon as we get used to each other, it gets a little boring and energy builds up again. It wants to move and it can't because we're locked into a relationship. Eventually the relationship explodes because we can't take it anymore.

I'll tell you about that process. When you meet somebody who's somewhere near the right vibration, or looks right, chemicals are released in your system to make a locking in. It's a biological thing so that you can reproduce. The chemicals are so strong that you become infatuated, you fall in love. What this means is that these chemicals form a film over your eyes, and you don't see the other person really clearly. You think this is the perfect person and it's because you don't see them. You have fallen in love. You don't see them and so they're wonderful, they're perfect and there's nothing else in the world! Then slowly these chemicals wear off and then the very things that were endearing now become annoying or irritating. You don't want to be around this person but you've made some sort of contract, so you hang in there.

All the time you're hanging on after the initial rush is over, you're wasting time. You need to move and move and move until that backed up sexual energy evens out. When it does, then you're not compelled and when you meet the opposite sex you're not hooked. If you keep moving like that, then the maturity and the balance happen. When your relationship breaks up, what you usually do is look for somebody else and get locked in again. You don't do the moving around you need to do. Keep doing that moving and you'll mature. You will start to meet people who are more mature and so the whole energy moves up until you reach this place where you become balanced. If you're with somebody, it's beautiful; if you're not, it's still beautiful. All the time you're locked into a relationship, you're not available to other people. You're suppressing something which builds up which will want to take revenge at some time.

Every time you've got backed–up sexual energy, you don't see your partner. If you keep moving, the energy evens out. By this I'm not talking about sex disappearing,

I'm talking about a natural balance being there. Then, when I meet you, I don't need you. If I don't need anything from you, then I can see you. If I can see you, then I can meet you. Jesus had a cute way of saying it. "When you see a man as a woman and a woman as a man, then will you enter into the Kingdom of Heaven." What he meant was that when you see a person, you are never clouded by desire.

Chohan: What is the importance of intimacy in relating?

Paul: Most people aren't intimate even when they're having sexual intercourse, because they are not there. That's because there's so much tension and so much going on in the mind with holding, inhibition and conditioning.

In fact, most people are never there. They're always thinking, "Am I doing it right?" Or, "Am I getting what I want?" There's all this activity in the mind and because of that there's no intimacy. Intimacy happens when the person disappears. It is there when this sexual energy has evened out and when there's nothing you need. You may become interested and you feel an invitation from yourself or the other to play, but you don't need it.

What that means is this. If you meet someone to whom you're attracted, and you feel that attraction, you're ready to follow it. If for some reason that person is not available, you move away and nothing is left, it means your energy is balanced. If you keep thinking about that person, if you see images of them or have fantasies, it means your energy is not balanced. You didn't see them. You just saw your fantasy of them.

When all that is gone and you don't need anything, then you're intimate the whole time. You're intimate with the chair. As you're touching it, you feel it. You're intimate with every person in the room whether they know it or not, because you're here and you're choiceless and you're available. You don't have any conditions inside you that say, "Even if I'm attracted to that person, I'm not going to be with them." You're saying, "I'm here. What's appropriate? I'm choiceless. What's available? What's not available?"

I'm not just talking about somebody to whom you're attracted, I'm talking about somebody you just meet. I'm talking about being there when you go across a border and there's a customs officer. You are there choicelessly. You've become choiceless because you've followed every single energy that's pulled you anywhere. You've gone, you've allowed it, you've never got stuck. Your relationship's finished, you're grateful and you move on. You keep moving and then something settles. You're intimate everywhere, and only then does love happen. All these other things are just infatuations, they're just chemicals. It's not love. Love is totally without conditions.

You do not love a person. It isn't love if you love them. Love happens and when it does, it happens everywhere in everything. You are love. You move in love. It's like a flower that's allowing its perfume. And then there's intimacy.

Chohan: Could you say something about the importance of honesty in order to attain this opening, this intimacy?

Paul: There isn't another way, you can't get there without honesty and most people don't know what that means. When most people are talking, there are levels of things going on. There is the social conversation, then there's something that goes on under that, and then again something under that. Maybe the next layer, the person is slightly aware of, but the layers beneath that they don't even know about. As you know, what we've trained ourselves to do here is to become aware of these different levels that are going on. There's the level of attraction, then there's a level of fear about that. Then there's another level, and beneath that another. It's about acknowledging these.

What we've done here as a technique is to share that. I say, "Now, I'm feeling attracted to you. Something in me wants to be with you." Then when I tune into that, I find that I'm afraid. Then, when I look at the fear, I find something else. We've learned to share that. When you do that, the barrier that's in between you and the unshared dialogue starts to melt and then an intimacy begins to happen.

Chohan: My final question concerns your vision of the future. I'm assuming you have one! Consciousness on this planet is going through a radical change and I'm wondering if you have a feeling of how relating or relationships are going to be a part of that change or opening?

Paul: In the most recent planet that you and I were on, a dimension called Venus (not the planet Venus), we existed nowhere and in nothing until we felt to be or were drawn to be. Then we would take on a slightly different vibration that formed us into another level of consciousness. When we didn't do that, there was no separation whatsoever, there was only the One.

But in the One there can be no awareness of the Self because there is only the One. In this dimension that we go back to, in between our sojourns to different planets, we're going to this place where there's nothing. Occasionally, we draw ourselves into ourselves and then sometimes for the fun of it we want to share that with somebody else. These two energies blend and become an ecstasy that this planet doesn't understand. It comes from a place of letting go of what we call ourselves, our personalities and our characters because those are not who we are. That is a very gross conditioning, a shell we've built around something that is so much finer.

What's going to happen on the planet is that many of the levels of what we call reality are going to change. At the moment, there's a storm raging here that is very wild and powerful. One hit England recently that destroyed 1,500,000 trees. There are changes in weather patterns, the whole economic situation is in a state of flux. AIDS is spreading faster than anyone could have imagined and other new diseases are starting to appear.

The planet is starting to say, "Let go of what you call reality, just let go and you will be somewhere else. There is no need to work on yourself anymore, or to go through things. Just let go and you will be somewhere else." At the moment, the present level of holding onto relationships is getting in the way of that process. Being with each other intimately without holding is in favor of that process, but you have to be available. We have to stop holding everything. And you know what I'm talking to you about now, especially in the inner team. It's about letting go of what you call reality, and how you see things. A chair is only a chair because you think it is. I'm encouraging you to let go and let go. When that happens, people are going to find that they do not go into this terrible place they're expecting.

The fact is that most people who are not in a relationship are not in let–go, they're in contraction. They're not in a relationship, because they're not worthy or they don't have someone to support them. If you let go and don't have a relationship in expansion, you're in bliss. Then in that bliss, and in that beautiful place, you can meet people unconditionally. You can have a relating that may only happen as a glance of an eye, but it will be more powerful than the most passionate sexual experiences that people are having now.

As you know, in this house, when we pass each other, we just look, and there's a tremendous experience. It's because there's an openness and an availability. It releases other levels of energy and vibration that are just waiting. If we let go and we keep doing so, reality as we know it will totally change. Sexual intercourse won't be the crude affair it is at the moment. It will be two people totally being in each other, being each other, and I know you must have felt that. There are some times when you are so connected with your beloved that sexual intercourse feels like it's in the way. Then what you want to do is disappear into the other and become the other totally, not that separation. There's a pain in separation. There's a pain, and you feel love for this other, and you want to be this other.

It happens with a tree, with a cat or with a flower. You see them being themselves and you feel so frustrated that you're separate. If you've learned to let go and let go when you look, the looker disappears and you become one with what you're looking at. Then another level of vibration happens.

Eventually, that's the way you become One with God. You stop seeing God as separate. It's very frustrating to see anything as separate.

Let go holding the definition of yourself and you'll become one with your beloved. If you go on allowing that, you'll become One with God. Then there's only One. And that's our possibility on this planet.

CHAPTER FIVE

MARRIAGE AND CHILDREN

An interview by Monny Curzon

Monny: People here talk of higher Selves and different dimensions and suddenly announce a surprising new name. I know that that's very ordinary for you, everyday chat or like cleaning your teeth. But then, these sorts of subjects get written down and circulars sent round to everybody and when one arrives, say in London, through the letter box with a tax demand, a couple of business letters and a picture postcard, then it does look rather extraordinary. It evokes mixed emotions.

What I'd like to ask you about are the sorts of mundane things which don't seem so extraordinary coming through London letter boxes. Every day topics like marriage and children and education and jobs, all the things that people at least claim are their great concerns. Since you have two delightful daughters, perhaps we could start with marriage and I could ask you how that fits into your view of things.

Paul: We have to go back to the extraordinary to start with. If we look at things the way you are saying, together with the business letters and the tax demands, then we have to look at everything the way everybody looks at everything, and that is not reality. We've been told that many times. The majority of the world claims to be religious, yet those that claim to be religious are not listening to the people who started the religions.

Let's take Christianity, which is closest to most people in the West. Jesus is quoted as saying, "Unless you leave your father, your mother, your sisters, your brothers, your wives and your children, you will not enter into the Kingdom of God." That isn't mentioned very much and he's also said many other things that people are not following, yet they pretend that they are basing their lives on some sort of religion. The masters, the people who knew, said that life is not what you think it is. "You need to wake up to reality. You've gone to sleep. You are not who you think you are. You are much more, you're not a miserable sinner, you are a Christ; you are a God. But you've forgotten that, you've gone to sleep and we've come here to remind you."

A few people round these masters started to feel that, they started to feel that vibration in themselves, to realize that they are more than they've been taught they are. They started to wake up, and then the master died or was killed, and then people started to worship him and then they no longer listened. They didn't listen because that energy wasn't there to keep reminding them, so then they went back to being children again, which is what the majority of people are.

That's even official. When there was a test in the UK for people who were being called up to fight in a war , the

IQ or the intelligence tests said most people are around twelve years old in their intelligence. They are not developing and they are not growing because they haven't had the encouragement to do that.

This planet is not working. Marriages get shorter and shorter, children get more and more violent. If we are honest with ourselves, we know that our society isn't working. It's reflected in everything: the weather, pollution, the state of the air, the state of the trees. We're in the Black Forest at the moment and I have heard that government figures show that sixty percent of the trees in this area are dying because of acid rain. We're killing the planet because of our ignorance.

There is another level and that's what the Masters have come along to tell us. If you don't tune into that, then eventually the planet will be destroyed.

Let me come back to marriage. Marriage as we know it is a very ugly institution. What it really means is one person trying to possess another. We often act that way too, whether we're in marriage or not. We try to possess the other because we don't feel complete in ourselves. We haven't looked for ourselves, we haven't found out who we are. When we do we know, we don't need anybody or anything. When we have matured, we feel our completeness and we're delighted to be on our own. If somebody else comes along in that level of maturity, we are delighted to be with them also.

If you want to get married for tax reasons or some other reason, then that can be done, but the hearts need to connect. Usually in a relationship, they don't, it's just the chemicals connecting. It's just a biological thing that happens in each system that says, "Get together to reproduce." The person isn't clear enough, isn't mature enough, to watch the whole system and that's why there's the honeymoon and then the disappointment. When the person has found himself they are then able to see the other and are more likely to be with a suitable partner. Then a marriage can happen. It doesn't have to be signed and officiated; a marriage of the heart can happen. It's a recognition of each other. At the moment, what we call marriage is just lassoing each other, saying, "Look, after the honeymoon's over, after the glory of seeing each other in what is actually rather a false way is exposed, we are still together so we can still hang on for whatever reason."

Monny: It is said that staying together has a certain abrasive creativity, a sort of Gurdjieffian type of meditation.

Paul: If people are aware of it, then every single situation is an opportunity. The reality is, however, that most people aren't. Just as you were asking that, something came through to talk about.

It's a story that somebody told me about a very famous horse breeder. His principle is not to put the best thoroughbreds together, but to let the horses choose their mates for themselves. In other words, they fall in love. He has been one of the most successful breeders of all time. Unlikely horses have gotten together and produced the most beautiful and successful foals, because they came together from their hearts. When an offspring is reproduced through the heart, you can tell. Somebody else was telling me that is what they have seen about India, that Indian people are ugly, they are ugly in their looks and their ways. That's one of the countries that has arranged marriages, they're not from their hearts. We keep trying to arrange things and do things and all we produce is ugliness. There is a place in us which we call intuition, but it's something else, there's a place in us that "knows." When we listen to that, beauty happens.

Monny: I think you're a bit hard on the Indians, although the point is very sound. Would you see in a future community that horse breeder's approach being the best?

Paul: What happens is everybody is sexually repressed, even young people who live in so–called freedom. The conditioning is always there. It's in the air, it's in our genes, it's everywhere.

There are a few tribes around the world that still encourage their children to be together at the right age. If we don't move the sexual energy, it backs up in us. We might be with somebody who is very beautiful, but this energy starts to want to move and it begins looking around, especially in men. The man is the hunter. If you are really given permission from the outside and the inside, if you really say experiment and go wherever you are attracted and play and have fun, this energy settles.

This settling is maturity. Then you start to meet somebody with whom you can go deeper and this is very helpful. When you truly and genuinely connect with somebody, and you want to go deeper with them, it happens on its own. You are not looking anywhere else in that way. You're open everywhere else, but the energy doesn't move. Then you go deeper and deeper, and when you do that, you find different depths in yourself and in the other. That does help maturity and it helps to see other levels of yourself.

Monny: Of course the outside world, the sort of harsher viewing people may tend to see matters back to front. They see youngish people leading a rather harum scarum sort of life and take all sorts of dire opinions. Would you see that as a preparatory phase for something resembling monogamy?

Paul: I see that as a possibility. But the trouble is, what's happening with the younger people is a reaction and it's not done out of consciousness. It's done out of rebellion, because they are not given permission by society. What they are doing is fighting the establishment, and there's no consciousness developing from that. What I'm talking about is not teaching anybody anything, but helping them to teach themselves, to say, "How do you see this? Sit down and look at it. Take a look at the pressures and then see what's happening inside of you. What do you want to do?" Not teaching them anything, but encouraging them to expand themselves, stopping the contraction and saying, "Look for yourself. What would you like to do? What feels natural for you?"

If they start to move around with that sort of consciousness, then each contact will be a love contact, and not just throwing out energy. Not just masturbating in the other, but really connecting with him or her. Something moves and a maturity happens.

What's happening at the moment is not going towards maturity because it's unconscious and in rebellion.

Monny: What about babies? Having children and plugging along with the spiritual path are not terribly compatible. How do you see that resolving itself, if at all?

Paul: Eventually it will resolve itself, but at the moment it's not appropriate. What that means is that the world and each person is in such a mess, that what they are doing is bringing a child into a handicap that's almost impossible. Most people have children unconsciously. They usually give more thought to buying a new car than having a child. With a child they don't think that much. It's too automatic. They just think that's what you're supposed to do, and if you don't have a child you are going against the flood. I don't see it as a free choice with most people.

The next thing I see is that most people have children because they are not complete within themselves. If they are totally complete, they don't need a child. Usually they do it out of some sort of compulsion. If the woman is unconscious, she's just listening to her biology, which is urging her to reproduce. If she's conscious, she can see the biology and she can see her consciousness, and then she can make a clearer choice.

We are so ignorant on this planet. A comparatively clear being comes into the world, and we just put our ignorance upon this being. We give it such a handicap that it makes it almost impossible. I am not saying that children are born clear because practically all children are born with karma. A few are not, for instance those that have decided to come into this level to help the change in consciousness, but most children are born as a result of past lives and therefore they are carrying things. But what we do to them is horrific.

I used to do some experiments with this. I used to get a hard bench and teach a subject that was not very interesting to people in a closed room for a very long length of time. Most adults just couldn't stand it, they went crazy. But that's what we force on our children. We force an education in a very unenlightened way and in very unpleasant conditions. We torture our children.

We get angry at work because our boss has been insulting to us, so we come home and take it out on the children. Then we might see what we are doing and close up, and the child doesn't get the love and the attention it needs. We give them such a handicap, and that's because we are not mature and we act out of our ignorance. If people are really awake and aware and they look at life through their own eyes and not through other people's, they will mature themselves. Then they can come to a place where there's really a clear decision. "Do I want to share what's happened to me with another being? Do I want to help them to do whatever they need to do in a loving and a caring way?"

Monny: But what would your horse breeder say to that? He's thinking, "Who's going to win the Derby in four years time?" In a community that is much more mature and is working to achieve true maturity, isn't it almost an obligation to have children who will benefit from this, who will hopefully be less batty than the others?

Paul: Well, I know that you don't have children. Most people who haven't had children don't know anything about them. When the child comes out of the womb it's not complete. In order to survive, it sucks. It sucks on the breast, it sucks on your energy, on your time, on your concentration. It wants you and it wants everything around it. It wants. That's the way it survives. If you are trying to find your maturity, trying to meditate, trying to realize who you are, this child is against you. There's nothing wrong in the child doing that. That's the way it needs to survive. Then it isn't just food it wants, or being kept clean, it wants your love and your attention and it wants them totally. When you are on the spiritual path, it takes everything, and that's why so few people have become realized. "Seek ye first the Kingdom of God and all else is added on to you." It has to be first. Again, if you reach a certain level of maturity, you've reached that through being totally devoted. You can still get married. You can still have children. You can still have your job, but your seeking is first. Usually you can't do that and have a child. It's impossible and it's not fair to the child.

Monny: Yes, with such a radical shift in the system of priorities, the constraints, the aims of normal society clearly go out of the window. I'm thinking of another department for the sort of average Londoner behind his postbox. He's off to work, often she's off to work too. How can people work in a way that is, as the Buddhists talk of, right thinking, right doing, all those? Everyone knows that it's fairly cut–throat in modern offices and the like.

Paul: We need to talk about various levels of this. First of all, usually the Buddhist went into a monastery. In the monasteries there were very few women so the men were cut off in every way. They cut themselves off from sex, and from normal life. They became what I call very boring people. Even when they woke up they were boring. They didn't have that juice of life and didn't understand people because they had avoided life.

How I see this planet is that we chose it in its entirety, and we didn't come here to cut ourselves off. We wouldn't have come here in the first place if we were going to do that. We came here to experience and enjoy everything.

When you are going into a new project you need to give yourself, to start with, as few handicaps as possible, make it as easy as possible. Later on it's different. It's fun to see how many handicaps you can give yourself and still retain your center.

To start with, make as few handicaps as possible. That might mean spending some time in a spiritual community, even if it's only two weeks holiday, maybe a little more time if you can, just to get started. Be in a place where people live who have already built up something. You walk into that atmosphere and you catch something much faster than you would otherwise, so you get started more quickly.

The next thing is, you meditate every day, without exception. Now, I use the word meditate. The way I see it is just sitting. Each day you spend some time sitting, doing nothing else. Then every now and again you go to a weekend or another concentrated time of sitting or being with people who are in this process. The next thing that is going to happen is that all the people who want to realize who they are are going to have to start coming together in small communities. On your own it's not possible, the pressure of the world, the pressure of the work is too much. You get too contaminated when you're out there.

If you come back to a small circle of friends with whom you are in tune, and you just sit down together and share what has happened for you during the day, it's going to be much easier than doing it on your own. You can spend a little time in silence and take turns cooking dinner. You can go deeper more quickly in a beautiful, supportive environment.

This is going to be the way, in small communities where you have this support, this love, this caring. Then you can go out and you can see how long you can hold that consciousness in the world. When you can do that, it is yours. As you know, we have a community here, and quite a few people have been out since the Six Month Project ended. They have come back and we're going out again after this six week seminar because it's no good staying permanently in a totally protected environment, because you don't know whether it's yours yet. You have got to go out and see. Do you still keep it after a few hours in the town? Do you still keep it after a few days in the world? You may lose it for a while, and you come back and you need to charge up again. Eventually you have to be able to have that wherever you are and whatever you're doing. So I don't see working in the world against this process. In a way, it's supportive of it. It does need more devotion from you. It does need more attention to remembering who you are in these situations.

Monny: Yet those little communities would not be exactly proselytizing other than through example. You don't really hold with any form of proselytizing do you?

Paul: Well usually what happens when somebody does that is they are talking about something that they don't know themselves. They are saying, "He told me." It's usually a man, very rarely a woman. "He told me this and I know it is the truth. He is the guru, he is the Master; so it must be the truth." You don't have to say anybody else said it, you can say, "This is my experience." As soon as you quote somebody else's words as your truth, you are lying. If you say, "Somebody else said so, I trust this person, I have a great respect for this person, and this person said this," that's not a lie. You're quoting the person. If you're saying, "That is so," like the people that knock on your door with the Bible, you are lying. They do not know this is so and you can tell that by their vibration which is violent. When somebody is talking with love and peace, you don't feel any violence, you don't feel anything being pushed at you. It's just like when a flower opens its petals and you can smell the perfume, or not. Any sort of pushing usually comes from ignorance.

As soon as you are realized, you realize that this person has also realized, but they haven't realized that they are realized. Just by your being, you might be a reminder. You might just say some little thing, but you never push because that's violent. So each small center or community has to be true to itself.

For example, my truth may be that I have met somebody who looks as though he's more awake than I am. It looks like more is happening for him than for me. In that case whatever he suggests I take as a hypothesis. When that happens in me it becomes my truth and then I can share it as my truth.

So any sort of missionary work I find ugly. I've lived in Africa and I've seen this missionary work in practice and I find it very ugly. It's not that there aren't some beautiful people there doing beautiful things, it's the overall concept that is ugly.

Monny: Undoubtedly, listening to Jehovah's Witnesses through the entry phone is a funny experience. And the way you suggest seems more natural or organic. But the spread of, or the contagion of this feeling, is that not contradicted by all the other darker influences that are rampant in society?

Paul: I remember a telephone call we had yesterday from somebody who did our Six Month Project. When she first came to be with us, she was a very neurotic woman. She'd been an actress and lived in different parts of America with what you might call the typical affected manner of the Hollywood film star. But she had a very beautiful heart and that's why she was accepted for the project. Slowly, slowly, something started to happen to her, without therapy, just by being in that atmosphere. Now this person has gone back to New York and everybody's started to ask her what has happened to her. Things are now starting to happen around her. What she's doing is sharing her experience, not what she heard or what she thinks is right, but sharing with people what happened to her. People are listening and they are coming together and they are starting to sit with her. People who would never think of sitting, never dream of being attached to a cult or one of these strange groups. They are attracted just because this person has transformed. They can see that the stress and the tension and the drive that were there before have settled, and they want that for themselves.

Now how that can happen in a big way at the moment I don't know. I'm living from moment to moment. What I'm seeing is, if enough people really say, "I want that," then maybe our team will go there and we'll have another course where more people can start to get it, and then it can spread.

It is going to spread. It's going to because many people are here from other dimensions, from other planets, from other places. They've come here because there is a transition happening to this planet and everything is going to become easier for the person who wants it. Conversely, it's going to become more difficult for the people who don't.

Everything is going to dichotomize. More people are going to do crazy things like spraying people with machine guns, or putting poison into aspirin bottles, or shooting people on the highways. There's also going to be more loving and more caring, more understanding and less judgment. That is because the very atmosphere of this planet is changing. Many unesoteric people, even people who scoff, can feel that this planet is changing. Even if you want to look at it in a very ordinary way, it's dichotomizing. There are more people meditating, there are more people being violent. What's happening is an energy is coming to the planet. It's neutral, so if you are expanding, if you are looking to be more loving and more caring, it'll happen very easily. If you are fighting and resisting, if you want to stay in control and in power, then you are going to feel worse and worse.

Monny: Stirring times!

CHAPTER SIX

AGING AND DYING

An Interview by Clare Soloway

Clare: I would like to talk to you about old people. With our work we don't have very much contact with people who are aging and getting to that point in their lives. I was hoping through this interview to have a look at why that is, and to see what you could say that might be of help to that particular group of people.

At the end of this century over half of the population in America will be sixty–five or over and a lot of them will be in old people's homes and waiting to die.

Paul: The way you're talking, what you want to do is the same as everybody else, work on the symptoms. You can go out and work on billions of symptoms, but the source remains the same. All the time you're working on the symptoms the source is producing more for you to work with. So you're trying to work on a huge circle, instead of coming right to the center and finding out why people get old at all.

People get old because they've been taught that they get old. People get old because they want to die. People want to die because their lives haven't been beautiful. They've had moments, they've had small things, but they haven't been encouraged to really live. They've been boxed in religions, in countries, in ideas, and they live in these boxes. And they rot in there.

While their energy is young enough to move, life is bearable, but when that energy isn't there anymore they start to collapse.

They do this because all the things they have suppressed, all the things they've wanted to do, all the things they've wanted to say, were pushed inside, and they rot there. The being rots so they become vegetables. When you say that I'm not working with them, that is because they have gone so far down, I can't get their spark back in a way that the spark will come back in others. So I'm working with people who are young enough, who have enough energy to wake themselves up to who they are. When they've awoken, then they can wake other people up to who they are, and they can work with them. When we have enough, we can start working, but we've got to start right at the source.

That is, we are not taught to live, we're taught to die. We're taught to fight death, we're taught to survive. Surviving is fighting death and you can't fight death. You're going to die, so it's hopeless. Most people, especially those in old people's homes, are pretending that they are not going to die, because they haven't been encouraged to get ready for dying.

How do you get ready for dying? You live. You live so totally you don't care whether you die or not because life is so important to you. You live. When you live that much, you really don't care whether you die or not. You've lived so completely, so totally, you're ready for whatever the next thing is. If it's death, good, anytime. To be ready for death you've got to live. To live, you've got to be ready to die any moment, you've got to be ready to die to everything. If this relationship is over, die to it. If this job is finished, die to it. When you've finished with the children, die to them, kick them out and let them start living on their own. This whole planet has been mollycoddled so much that people start to die the moment they are born. They're so protected by conditioning, they're dying. They're not living. They are not expanding. Everybody's contracting with survival: "How am I going to take care of myself and those around me?" How to keep this off, how to keep that off, to be safe, instead of saying, "What is this about? What is this planet about?" You didn't come here to survive, just to keep yourself together until you've got enough money to die. You're going to die. Everybody's going to die.

We've got to bring death into our lives the same way we bring life, the same way we bring adventure in, more so because nobody's really adventurous. Sex needs to be mentioned more, death needs to be mentioned more, all the taboos need to be burst open. Religion has covered these things over because that's the way it can control you. It controls you because you are afraid of sex. It controls you because you are going to die and you don't want to die. We have to burst all these bonds, burst through everything we've been told and say, "I want to live, what does it mean to live?" Then, when old age comes, you won't be old. You'll still be full of life until the body says, "Now I need to go home." As you are lying down you will say, "Body go home any time you are ready." If you really, really live, you are ready to die.

When you are ready to die, you will realize nobody ever gets born, and nobody dies. It's an illusion, it's an idea.

You get popped into this body because you need the experiences. Each person is just the same as God. God was never born, God will never die, God is and you are. The body gets born. You come in with it and you live in there. You live in the restrictions of the body and you can play and have fun if you want to. The body will die but you won't, you will just pop out. If you need another body, you'll pop into another one. If you don't, then you'll enjoy the next dimension.

Clare: When you are talking I'm getting really excited about living and I'm forgetting all my questions about dying and people getting older. I was thinking how just in that moment you made me enthusiastic about living, about being alive and how our work is that. Do you see making people enthusiastic about life as a part of your work?

Paul: That's what this plane is, an adventure. It is planned as that. Adventure does several things: it keeps you amused for a while, it stretches your resources, it develops you, it matures you and it expands you. This whole planet was designed for that.

The trouble with old people is that nobody told them. They were put into school and were told, "This is it," by people who didn't know anything. Not so long ago, we were teaching that the world was flat, then we changed it. Now it's round. Every few years, we completely change our minds about the most basic things. The truth is we have no idea about anything.

The scientists are starting to get there. They are beginning to see that nothing is how it looks, but that hasn't reached the schools or universities yet. We're being taught archaic things and it is all to box us in and say, "This is it."

What we need to say is, "We don't know what is it." Nobody knows what's it. We have no idea what it is.

We start breaking an object down through magnification and we find there's something else in there. Then we find that there are millions of those in there, and we haven't found the final anything. Every time the scientists have a breakthrough, all that happens is that they find something else even smaller.

We really don't know anything about anything. But we're not taught that in school. We are taught, "This is it." We're boxed. There's no adventure, no room for expansion. Of course these old people are rotting, of course they are senile, of course they have no lives of their own. If there's enough change in consciousness with people like you and me, they'll catch it. Then they'll run their own homes, they'll have the doctors and nurses there to take care of their bodies but they will run their own lives.

Eventually, there will be teams of people going into the homes and saying, "Your old age is an illusion. You are not old. You are not young. You are never born and you'll never die. You are, and you know that." Each person knows that, if they sit, if they are awake enough, there's somebody in there.

Who's watching?

Who's looking?

Who knows they are old? Somebody can watch all that. The one who watches isn't old, the one who watches is. As soon as the person starts to identify with his watcher, it doesn't matter what goes on in the body, it's just a machine to him. It's either in good condition or it's not. The watcher is alive, the watcher is eternal, the watcher is God, the watcher is love. We need to disconnect and to help other people disconnect from what they are clinging to. If they disconnect, they will find that they are not the body, they are not the mind, they are not the emotions. They are God.

Clare: As I'm sitting here I realize how incredibly privileged I am, how lucky I am to be who I am and to have the opportunity to be in touch with the sort of things that I'm in touch with. Then I think about my parents ...

Paul: It's nothing to do with luck. First of all let's look at this. You accept that there are other lives but most people are terrified to accept that. You know now that you have been in other lives and you have been ready to accept that.

In other lives, every time you have been given the choice of the light or the darkness, mostly you have chosen the light. It's nothing to do with luck, there's no such thing as luck. The universe lives in balance, everything's in balance. Every time you choose the light you are more light, every time you choose the darkness you are choosing to be more darkness. When you talk about your parents, you treat them as victims. Nobody is a victim, nobody. Everybody is exactly where he is, right now, because that's not only what he has chosen, but where he is choosing to be moment to moment.

This old illustration comes to me. You remember when you and I were in Africa, we were working with starving Africans and the Red Cross, and wanted to take them to another valley where there was water. They wouldn't go because they felt their tribe and tradition would be devalued. They chose to die rather than move to where they could live. They chose that. Each person is choosing his or her life right now.

Your parents are choosing that, and it's an accumulation of every choice they've made not to be in the light.

They chose to be in survival, they chose money. They didn't choose meditation, or the light. If they had, they could wake up now. The trouble is they have given themselves such a burden. With every one of these choices for survival, they've burdened themselves and it is very hard to snap out of it. But nobody is a victim, anybody can snap out.

The woman who's raped is not a victim. The person who is injured in a car accident is not a victim. Each of them has created that. We are creating everything that is happening to us right now, but we don't want to admit that because we don't want to be responsible.

"It happened to us." Nothing happens to us. We create it. Every single negative thought you have is creating darkness in your life. Every time you have a judgment in a way you can't understand, you are changing the molecules. You are changing something that is going to come back and say, "This is your balance with that thought."

When you are responsible, you will wake up. There's no karma, there's no balance. You live in the light, because you live in awareness. These people who are in old people's homes have chosen that. They chose that because that's what they need. They chose it before they were born. Before they were born, they said, "This is the life I need to learn what I need to learn, to balance what I need to balance." The trouble is, you get into this life and you forget, then you are a victim. You complain and when you do that, you make no balance. You don't balance off anything, you just build up more. You die, and as you die your life passes before you.

You see every time when you were unconscious, every moment you were in the darkness, you know that you have got to come back and put it right.

Now there's another aspect to this, nobody has to put anything right, all you have to do is repent. Repent doesn't mean, "I'm sorry for myself." Repenting turns round, erases the situation and says, "Right, that's gone, be aware of it and it's finished." No balancing is necessary. Wake up and there's nothing to balance. Every person who is suffering in an old people's home at the moment has chosen that. They chose it consciously in another dimension and have chosen it here through their unconsciousness. If they had awakened, if they'd put their main energy into waking up, they wouldn't be in that home. They'd be surrounded by loving people. They would be living exactly the way they wanted to live.

We have to wake up to who we are, and that's what we came here for. A whole team of us who have been round many planets in many lifetimes has come back to wake up and remind people.

Buddha tried it, Jesus tried it. Many people have tried it. It wasn't quite the right time then. There wasn't the right reception. Now it has to be. If this planet is going to survive, we have to help people to wake up to who they really are.

Clare: When you talked about victims, I realized something for myself about my parents. I find that I get hooked into them and feel guilty. I really love them and I feel their pain and it tears me.

Paul: Pain is resistance. Your form of loving is not love, it's just sentimentality. I have hammered my parents all their lives with one thing or another. I have been relentless and never given in to them. I have written letters that have totally shattered them. I have done things that have blown their lives apart. My love for them has always been there, but I have never given in to their sentiment or their stupid and restricted ways. I said, "This is my truth, this is the light as I see it, and I am not listening to you because the example of the way you are living is no example to me. That is not the light, that is ignorance. I am not coming to your ignorance."

I held this position that looked cruel for years. Now something has clicked, they have woken up and now they see. In fact, my mother probably understands what I am doing as much as anyone else on this planet, not intellectually but she knows what I am and what I came for. She knows I am not of this planet. The only reason she got to that is that I never gave in to her weakness. I just kept telling her the truth until something clicked and she heard it.

What your parents do is try to pull you down all the time. They say, "I am a victim, look at me, poor me." They pull on your sentiment. You have got to have the courage to say, "No." You have got to hammer them. They might get angrier and cut you out of their will again. You have to have the courage to say, "This is the truth, I know this is the truth. You can accept it or reject it." It might put them into more pain. Pain is resistance. They do not want to hear what the truth is, they want security. They want to be safe. Their lives aren't working, most people's lives are not working. Their whole lives are based on survival and security. Who is secure? Nobody feels secure. As you know, we have worked with billionaires and even they are not secure. While your life is based on security you can never feel secure. Give it up and you are secure. You are here, you are now.

Clare: I was just realizing that one of the things that is absolutely remarkable about you is you're uncompromising. Could you talk about this part of yourself that is so strong and sometimes seems so ruthless?

Paul: What you call compromising is sentimentality. It's concern and not caring. It is about yourself and not about the other. For a certain time in anybodys life, if he or she wants to reach the light, they have to be totally selfish. Their lives have to be about them and nothing else. They have to look and look and look and not care or be concerned about anything else. If you keep doing that, you wake up. The moment you wake up, you move into caring and not concern. What most people call love is concern. What they really mean is, "I don't want you to suffer, because while you are suffering I feel bad." They don't even see the other. When you have spent enough energy on yourself and you realize who you are and you wake up, you say, "So that is what it is all about!"

This person is supposed to be suffering. If he weren't he would not wake up. He was supposed to have that car accident. He was so asleep that he was just wasting his life here.

You still care. When you see somebody suffering it touches you, but not in the way it touches other people who usually just feel uncomfortable. Until you see yourself, you cannot see the other. Whatever you experience is you. Until you have reached that place of clarity, you can't even begin to see the other. If you see anger out there, it is not someone else's anger you are seeing, it is your own. If you are clear of anger, you just see energy. If you see suffering out there, you think you are seeing it in someone or something else, but you are not. You are seeing your own suffering.

When you have learnt that, you see that everything is supposed to be happening just as it is. It is part of what people have designed for themselves, to help them to wake up. Most of what you call love is sentimentality. You won't reach love until you love yourself. When you love yourself, everything is love. It just takes another form. These people so loved themselves that in a place when they were free, free of a body, free of everything, they saw that they were not yet complete. They decided to go into that suffering to help to complete themselves.

Everything is love. When you have realized that for yourself, all you see is love. Until then, it is concern and sentimentality and it doesn't help the other. If you love a person enough, you will tell her the truth. What you say is, "I don't want to tell her because it will hurt her." She needs that. You don't tell her because if you tell her you think she won't love you.

You don't love yourself, so you need her love. You compromise, which is another way of saying you lie. Everyone is a liar, everyone is living in lies. There are very few people on this planet who are living in truth. When you meet them you will know because they shine. You will recognize them the moment they come in the door.

Every moment you know whether you are lying or not. Most of the time you go unconscious so you don't have to see when you are lying. You go into a cliche or you go into one of your habits or one of your addictions. That keeps you busy from seeing who you are at that moment. You need to say, "Am I in my truth this moment, am I having the courage to be myself this moment?"

Clare: Part of my adventure right now is having lost the topic that I started talking to you about earlier. However, I feel that I am very here with you.

Paul: For most old people it is too late. Their main drive has gone and they want to die, they want to get out, and be finished. There are some who are ready to look, but they don't know where to start, because what they have been taught does not work. The normal religions don't work. They are nothing, they are worse than nothing, they are teaching them lies. But it is not hopeless for anybody at any age, right until the last moment.

If a person is perfectly ready to die, there is hardly anything to say. It is just a sharing of energy. Even in the old person that energy is there. The truth is there, life is there, eternity is there. If a person has reached this state himself he will reawaken that energy. When a person is about to die it is a very good time to get that transfer over, because up until then he has been struggling to live. As he is starting to die he can see it is hopeless, that he has no control over life and death. At that moment, when he gives in he can catch it. If he catches it, he will die in a totally different way, which means that he may not have to be born again. Or if he is, he will be born in a totally different circumstance. This is because the work has to be done on this plane. It can't be done on the others.

You can't experience in the next plane. This is the level to experience, so every single second in this lifetime is important. That is why five billion people have rushed to this planet at this time and many more are trying to get here. This whole planet is about to take this turn in consciousness. Everybody wants to be here for it. The trouble is, with the whole birth process and your conditioning, you forget what you came for. We are here to remind people what they came here for, that's all. They will do the work themselves. We are not here to teach them anything or show them anything. As soon as they remember who they are and what they came for, they will do the work. They know exactly what to do. We all do, we have just had it conditioned out of us. Come back to who you are, disconnect from all this conditioning and you will remember why you came here. As soon as you remember you will do it, you will seek first the Kingdom of God.

You will train yourself to wake up because that is all you came here for. You will experience everything there is to experience, choicelessly. You won't bother about your families or your children or your money: they will all be second. Everything will be second to remembering who you are. That is what people say after a near death experience. They love their children more. They love their partners more. They are more conscientious at work. They are more balanced with their money and their possessions. But these are all secondary, because now they know their priorities. They are, "Seeking first the kingdom of God, and then all else is added on." Everything becomes a balance.

Our job is to wake up. First of all, you need to wake up and the only way you are going to do that is making it the most important thing in your life. As soon as you have woken up, you will remember who you are and then it is all over. You know who you are. From then on it is just fun, just having a good time, and in the process you will be helping others to wake up.

Clare: I am trying to catch what is the holding on as you are talking. As I sit here, there is absolutely nothing else, and then I see myself in an hour's time going back in to that holding place. I also see how this is with older people too.

Paul: The holding is that you are in a body which is programmed to survive. It is a machine and it has a survival chip in there, and so your energy gets caught up in that. You haven't seen yet that you are not the machine. The machine is part of you, but you are not it. You don't have to worry about survival, the machine needs to worry about that. That is why it has pain when it bumps itself. It is part of survival. It is supposed to be like that, but you are not like that. You are not the machine. You are God, you are freedom, you are everything that is in this machine. You have voluntarily trapped yourself in there in order to have the fun of untrapping yourself and finding out who you are. Many people are now getting out of their bodies. They just come out of their bodies and they say, "Here is the machine. While this machine is alive it has to be fed and it has to be looked after and it gets afraid of certain things. It enjoys certain things. It doesn't like pain, it enjoys sex. I'll take care of the machine but I am not the machine. I can come out whenever I want to." People can now just close their eyes and they are out. They can go travelling. That's only part of it because that still has to do with this dimension. There is another dimension when you don't travel that way, where you live in a higher place.

At the moment you go back when the machine says, "Survive." In order to survive you have got to know who you are, you have got to be careful about yourself and you realize you are not the machine. You say, "But this isn't who I am. I have lived many times. I have had many personalities and many characters and if I go on living in ignorance I will have many more personalities and many more characters."

When you wake up, you are free from the whole system. Then you make a choice. Some people will use it to heal physically because that is what their flavor is. Others will help people be free because that is their flavor. Other people will just dance, others will sing, others will paint, others will clean, others will do gardening, but the very flavor of their being will be healing. Whenever you see this person that fine vibration will awaken your vibration, and say, "Listen we are not trapped, we are God. We are eternity." You'll catch it. It won't be a thought, it won't be intellectual. You'll feel it. It'll wake you up and as you start to wake up you will say, "I want this, I don't want to live the other way." And then you will start saying, "How can I live in this?"

Your whole life will be about living in this energy, living in this light, living in this joy. Then you may decide you want to share it with other people. It is incidental. Each person creates his or her reality. They are responsible. It is demeaning to see it any other way.

Thus spake Sanat Kumara.

CHAPTER SEVEN

THE NEW PHASE

An Interview by Casey O'Byrne

Casey: I'd like to start this interview by talking to you about your past. You've spent twenty years in the growth movement. You've counselled thousands and thousands of people worldwide. You were at the peak of your career and then you just dropped it all, threw it all away for what you call the new phase. Could you tell us what the new phase is?

Paul: It's to do with something that's awakened in me. I am now seeing from a different level of consciousness and as I look from there, I see that everybody is capable of seeing from there. There is also something new happening to the planet. There's a new energy coming which is making things very different. In the past, we had to work through things. We had to complete things because there was karma. Now that's not necessary. We're coming to the end of this phase and all that is needed is a waking up. That's just awakening to who we are. The old methods of working through things are no longer appropriate because there's no time for them. It's got to be an awakening and now I know that's possible. It's happened in me and it's happening with the people around me. So instead of wasting time working through things bit by bit, it's a question of tuning in to the energy that's been created, listening, being open for a possibility that hasn't been available before, and letting it happen.

Casey: You say that self realization happened to you. How did that happen?

Paul: I'm not sure of the how. All I can say that's useful is that I made realizing my potential, finding out the maximum of which my system was capable, the most important thing in my life. Out of that I started to see other things that I was looking for.

To start with, it was skills and capabilities, and after that finding out what the mind would do. Then I discovered consciousness, and I wanted to find out how much I could expand my own consciousness.

Through that came the realization that we're not who we think we are, that in fact these things we've been told from the East, that the world is maybe a dream, are actually true and this is one small fragment of a dimension of the whole. In my searching, in my looking, in my intensity, I woke up to that fact.

Casey: It took you a long time to reach this stage. Now you have sixty people here at this villa, and in six months you're going to bring them to self–realization. In Zen it's twenty years, in Tibet, a lifetime commitment and there's no guarantee. How is it possible to do it in six months now?

Paul: There's no guarantee here. It depends on the in-dividual. I'm available and this expanded energy is avail-able. Also, there is a new energy on this planet available to each person. All that's needed is an openness. As you wake up, you realize that no time is needed, it's just a realization.

Nothing has to be worked through, all that can be done is a preparation. This happens automatically through con-sciousness. If you become more conscious of everything you do, everything you say, and everything you think, something starts to expand on its own. Then, in that ex-pansion, the realization happens. In the past we were told it takes that long, so we have assumed that it's taken that time, and we've worked with that formula. Now, in this new era, all that's needed is a preparation. If we are aware of everything we do, say and think, we become aware of what's most beneficial for us.

Then we will stop smoking, we are likely to stop eating meat and fish and we are going to have our negative and judgmental thoughts drop away. In other words, it be-comes a purifying process. Nothing has to be done, just awareness and you start to do these things automatically.

Casey: My experience of these sixty people who are here doing this process of purification, is that they are very or-dinary people, from all different walks of life. Is it possible for everybody to attain this?

Paul: It is possible, but it depends on how much covers their consciousness, how much conditioning is there. If there is a lot, then it becomes more difficult, although it's still possible. The people who came here had done a cer-tain amount of work, a certain amount of preparation, in this life and many other lives, so it's comparatively easy for them. What's going to happen as a result of this is, as these people wake up to themselves, it is going to become easier for other people to do the same, because others are going to see that it's possible. It's like Roger Bannister running the four–minute mile. As soon as he had done it, everybody knew it was possible, and then it became easier.

Casey: A little earlier, you talked about levels of awareness, levels of consciousness, and how awareness is one of the keys or techniques that you are using to get through. Are these techniques that anyone could use to obtain self–realization?

Paul: The main thing is for people to want it enough. If it's done as an aside, a hobby, it's not enough. Certainly, your life will improve and become more beautiful, but this realization happens through wanting it more than anything else. The main thing is, "I want to know who I am. I want to wake up!" Or, "I've read a book where people have had near death–experiences and I want to realize that without a life–threatening situation. If that's possible, I want it." Now if that's the most important thing in your life, everything else follows. You then start to become aware of everything you do. It's very simple, but at first not easy. You are just aware of what you do and what you say and what you think, choicelessly, so there is no judgment about it. "I thought that, I did that, I observed that." That's the basis.

Casey: So I'm a person living somewhere in North America. I have a family and a job and my bank account and my car and all those things. Do I need to drop all that to become self–realized?

Paul: You need to drop your attachment to it. If your family, your children, your wife, your job, your money is in front of your realization, that will be your barrier. You won't be able to go past that. That's survival. If you allow an opening for that, make your freedom the most important thing, and let go of your attachment to these other things, the energy will start flowing on its own. If you were to get rid of these things, as many people do, that's not finishing it. The attachment can still be there, whether you are with it or not. It's just realizing, "I'm attached to this. Unless this works out the way I want, I'm not happy." You look at that, because that is enslaving you.

You look at everything. In one way, nothing has to change and in another way, everything has to change. There does come a point where you need a certain amount of time, here it has been six months. The next experiment is six weeks, maybe we'll get it down to six days. There does need to be a time when the person is totally devoted to this in a supportive atmosphere, in an energy that has already reached this level of vibration, where the person can be total without outside distractions.

Casey: Okay, so he doesn't have to drop it, he just has to be aware of it, bring his consciousness to it and then his self–realization will come as a result of his awareness?

Paul: It will be available to him. Now, whether he takes it or not is another thing, because then, as he reaches this place, he realizes that if he makes this step, he steps out of this illusion that this is everything.

Casey: You talk about people creating their own realities. Why does someone create the reality of his mortgage and his overdraft at the bank, instead of creating the reality of self realization?

Paul: It's a matter of ignorance. Everything you do has an effect. Every choice you make has an effect. If you choose this way it has one effect, if you choose that way it has another. So if you insult somebody, that will have an effect because that person might tend to be against you or get you in some way. You have created something, so it has an effect. Everything you have ever done has an effect on your life.

You have also been conditioned and told the way things are and you believe that. You don't find out for yourself, you just believe it. Everything you think, everything you do, is creating your life.

If you come to somebody who has had this realization and you are open to them and you try to listen, and you experiment with their suggestions as a hypotheses, you might start to see that by disconnecting from these things, not by suppressing them, just disconnecting, life starts to happen magically in a short time. It's very difficult to explain, but every thought has an effect. A thought is a vibration and it affects things.

Some people can bend metal without touching it. Others can hold a watch and repair it just by holding it, just by thought waves. Everything we think, everything we do, every idea we have is affecting our lives. But then we get into negative patterns, one unpleasant thing happening produces an unpleasant thought, which in turn produces something else unpleasant. That's why I'm saying it's good to have a time out of everything for a while, to see things more clearly, to get the wheel turning the other way.

Casey: So you say, "Out of everything for a while." Like a retreat. The people here in this villa have been here for five months and they will be here for a total of six. You've condensed the information or guidelines that you've taken for the six months, and then I understand there is going to be a six week project. The people from the six months as well as the six weeks will leave this retreat type setting and they will go back to their lives, maybe New York City, maybe London or Tokyo. As everybody knows, these cities are like jungles. How does something as delicate as a person coming from this survive in a jungle like New York?

Paul: When my system stops resisting, it becomes transparent. When a noise comes, instead of the system resisting that noise and thus getting shaken by it, the noise comes, it shakes, it remains choiceless and the vibration goes through. You are shaken but you are not identified with that part of yourself.

Casey: To attain this level of transparency, there are things that we do here. We do sittings, we do something called tuning–in. Can you explain what these are to the layman?

Paul: Sitting is traditionally what has been called meditation, but sitting for me is just sitting with eyes open or half open, and allowing everything to happen that wants to happen, with no distractions. Out of that, a clarity comes, a quietness comes, a stillness comes, and then you start to be aware that there are other parts of yourself. You could call this your internal voice or your higher Self. They are all available. You can then ask questions and get answers.

After you reach a certain clarity, you become self– activating. You've done a certain amount of clearing. You can hear to a certain extent, and then you can just ask your higher Selves or entities or guides, whatever you call them, and you start to get your own answers. You are not distracted and you don't need anything from the outside. You know at this point that you have everything that you need. It's available to you from the inside and you see you are supported in many ways. You realize that there is more to this dimension, to this reality, than you have seen before. You see you are being taken care of, you are being loved, you are being looked after. All that's needed is to go inside, become still and listen. Ask your questions and you will get your answers.

What we are helping people to see is just what they have been told over and over again, "This is it. Thou art that." This is complete, and the more you look to the outside, the less you realize that. Don't follow anything, don't believe anything. Just listen to suggestions, take it as a hypothesis, take it inside and look for yourself. Then when you have these realizations, they are yours. It's not a matter of believing or disbelieving. It's happened. And then remembering that no matter what happens, that's always available.

If you slow down, become still, go inside and ask your questions, your answers will be there.

CHAPTER EIGHT

MONEY AND BUSINESS

An Interview by Roxi McNay

Roxi: What I've found in my life is, until recently, that I've had this driving force to be successful in the world and make money. That has probably been my most powerful motivating factor until the last year or two. Somewhere I always knew that when I had money, I wouldn't be happy, yet I had to make money to find that out. And it is so well documented, people like Howard Hughes and Jean Paul Getty who became very, very rich, and at the same time always had highly publicized, very unhappy lives. Yet making money, for virtually everybody, seems to be such an important part of their lives, even though they know somewhere that when they have it, they won't be happy. I wonder why that is?

Paul: There are several channels here that we are talking about. We're born with certain things within us and one is a very powerful instinct to survive. This system, this body, this mind, these emotions have a built in program that says survive, and you go through all sorts of things to survive.

There are incredible stories about people and what they've been through to do that.

One of the best ways to survive on this planet is to have money. If you have money it helps to take care of your system as much as possible, unless you make yourself ill getting the money. So that is one drive.

Then there is another drive, that is a drive of inquiry. There is a drive of adventure, a drive to know. What often happens is that these two things get lined up with each other. We'll leave that aside for a moment and we'll talk about something else.

People are born into this dimension, onto this planet, with different levels of consciousness, with different levels of attainment. Often child prodigies are, for example in music, famous past composers who have come back onto this planet and their skills are still there. Many people are born with great skills, great capabilities, because they have had this experience in previous lives. I know that to the average person past lives are not acceptable, but to intelligent people, anybody who's looked at it, or studied it, it's a fact and there's no way of denying it.

So some people are born with a great capability. Now what are they going to do with that? They come onto this planet, choosing a situation they need to go through, and they have all this energy and this drive to survive. They've got this drive of inquiry and these tremendous skills, so they put them somewhere. Some become great artists, some become great musicians and some become great businessmen.

If you look at the lives of these people, they are very similar because what they are doing is their total focus, anything else is secondary. Wives, relationships, possessions all come second. Even fame becomes secondary.

Now, they haven't had the exposure on a sufficiently powerful level to see that the energy in one way is being misdirected. It's being directed in a channel that can't be self fulfilling. It can't be; it's not supposed to be. The only thing that is self–fulfilling is self–fulfillment, and in self–fulfillment you have to be that total, that complete in saying, "Who is this? What is this? Where did it come from? Where is it going? What's going on with it moment to moment?"

If you bring the amount of energy that you put into the business to yourself, you realize who you are. Once you have realized who you are, you can have money if you want to. You can have your fame, you can have anything you want, once you are realized. You find your source and your source is the source of everything.

Roxi: When I started my business, I knew I would be successful although success wasn't coming straight away. Then I split up with my girlfriend and I was running a new business with no emotional support from a relationship. Although in one way it was very hard, something changed in me then, and the knowing became a total, "I am going to be successful." My sex drive and the energy I had in my relationship went totally into my business.

Paul: So that's illustrating what I said. You have this drive. The sex drive is survival but it also has a secondary part to it. It's an energy unto itself. It is a drive and it is an energy. So you've got your business and you've got your sex and maybe you have a family. Maybe you have possessions you have to take care of, valuable things that are fragile. They are all taking energy. If one of them isn't there, that energy can go into the business. If you are not using your energy in sex, the whole energy goes into something else.

If somebody is just mildly intelligent and total, they will become a multimillionaire. It's not to do with skills, it's to do with totality. If you are total, you'll be listening the whole time. You may not have the skills yourself, but you'll hear of somebody who has and you'll utilize theirs, because your whole energy is for that. If you disconnect from these things, that's where the energy goes.

Roxi: But it also seems to be a fact that some people are much better at making money than others. One of the things that I hear a lot is that people would like to do certain things in their lives but they haven't got the money. They can't afford it. They only have a regular income from a job and they want to travel the world. They want to have all the things that the rich people have. You were saying earlier that some people were born with certain abilities from past lives. What about the ones who weren't? It seems that there are a lot of people in the world who don't really have that ability to get rich.

Paul: Let's say they have the ability, but it's not developed. What people are born with are aptitudes. So it's easier for some people to do that than for others. Some people will never be a Segovia. It doesn't matter how many hours they practice at the guitar, they'll never be a master. But they could be very, very good. Anybody could if he has got the inclination to practice enough. The thing is, if it isn't total, it won't be enough. If somebody says, "I'd really like to play the guitar but I've got this and this to do." Then it won't happen.

You've just mentioned going round the world. I went around the world with a very small amount of money and the partner I went with actually had an overdraft when we set off. It isn't a matter of money. It's, do you want to go around the world?

I remember the time when it registered with me. I was giving a hitch–hiker, who was an East African Asian, a ride on the M1 in England. In his holidays from University he used to hitch–hike around the world. I was talking to him and I said, "Well how do you manage to get a shower every day and what does it cost?" As I was talking, I thought, "I can do that." So I did it. If you want it enough you do it, but you have to really want it.

Some people have aptitudes and it's easier for them, but anybody can do anything, providing he is not brain–damaged or does not have some physical damage that makes it impossible. Anybody can do anything if he wants it enough. What most people do is diversify too much. They are supposed to have a wife, and a family, and two cars, and a house in the country, and all these things. Then the energy is spread out and they are never total about anything.

Roxi: One of the things that I find in business is the level of honesty of many people is not very high. It varies, there are almost certain rules for certain levels of dealing. For example, it seems to be acceptable to be totally dishonest with the tax collector. On other levels the dishonesty may be more discreet. I'm just wondering how I can be totally honest and yet still maintain my level of success?

Paul: If you remember when you first came here, you were a businessman. You were successful but there was always the struggle around you. You were trying to attain something. Then you made various steps and one of them was to be here for six months and to totally leave your business. I don't know whether it's still so, but you used to say you were getting more success, there was more coming to you without the stress and the strain. With this release in you, something started to happen.

You say there are these levels of honesty. Honesty is not a transaction, it's an energy. It's not what we would normally call a fact. It's a feeling, it's a vibration. You know what's honest. And you know what is creating what could be called karma or a back pressure. You can feel it. You have become more honest and as you become more honest your business has become more successful.

Always there is something inside that says, "Should I go on?" Then in comes the gambler. Is your business more important or is your self–realization more important? When I talk about the truth I don't mean what people normally call the truth. I mean that energy that's clear and pure, that is not in any darkness of any sort. If you stay in that light, you'll become more and more successful, you'll get what you need. Now, it might not be in your business, because you might lose interest in that. It might be in something totally different. You'll be in the light, you'll be where you want to be. You won't be like those billionaires who become very unhappy with themselves. Whatever you'll be doing, that light will be with you.

When you are talking about whether to be honest or not, you are looking with the mind and you are looking into the future at a hypothetical situation. You know, since you have been here for six months, the more honest you have been with yourself, and incidentally with other people, the lighter your life has become. Now, have you got the courage to go on doing that, or is the pressure of five billion unconscious people going to pull you back? If it starts to pull you back, all you've got to do is look around among your fellow businessmen and that will be your life. If you want to look at something else in some other way, look at how you have been here, lighter and lighter. That's to do with the truth.

Roxi: You've talked a lot about the changes that are going to happen in the world. We are probably going to have a lot of physical changes in the planet with earthquakes and hurricanes and all kinds of things. I get a feeling of the new kind of society that will emerge from that. Do you have some idea of how business will be in a new kind of society? I'm just wondering how the new way of being will be for us, as conscious people working towards the light.

Paul: Business as it is now is a war. We condemn wars but there is a war in every business every day with very few exceptions. And the war is, "I get and you lose. I'll see how much I can get, and the more I get, the more you lose." And it's not based on love, of course. There are exceptions, there are some very beautiful businessmen. They may not be so internationally successful but that's mainly because they don't want to be. But they work in a very beautiful atmosphere.

I'm just remembering now that I went to the dentist yesterday. This is usually not a pleasant experience for my system. However, walking into that place was a totally different experience. It wasn't a business, it hadn't got that tension and coldness about it. The dentists were a man and his wife with some assistants working in a totally different atmosphere of caring. Now, I would imagine they are very successful. They are regarded as the best dentists in town, and they have very beautiful offices. But my feeling was not of them making money, it was that they are taking care of people, they are actually interested in people's teeth. I went to the hygienist and she did some work and told me the dentist needed to look. The dentist came and said, "I don't have time for this, but I think my wife does." And then he came back to see how she was doing because he was interested, he cared. There was this whole feeling of caring in there, I would call it love. They are successful and it looks like they are doing exactly what they want to do and they are really enjoying it.

Mostly business is a war, and it's a war because we have wars. We have generals who want wars because if they don't, they have no job. We have arms manufacturers who want the support of generals because if nobody wants a war, they can't make their ammunition. Then we go down the line and you say, "But that's not me." That's not true because everybody is in a war. Then you say, "My business is not."

Take a look inside. You've got a war inside, too. You might have a war with your wife or your children or your dog. "I should do this, I should do that, I shouldn't have said that, I should have done this." There is a war. What's going to happen with this change of consciousness is that we are going to manifest our internal state on the external. What is going on with us at the moment, we are going to project to the outside. We are already doing it. We pollute ourselves with our ideas, with our suppression, with our pornographic thoughts. We don't have the courage to follow what we want to do. The inside is on the outside, we are polluting the planet. We are all building up to something inside. We can feel it, and we are doing that on the outside.

The economy and the weather are doing it. The hole in the ozone, the atmosphere, AIDS are all contributing to it. Everything is reflecting what's on the inside to the outside. It's going to become so obvious that we are going to start to see that somewhere every individual on this planet is responsible for the world. We are creating it. We are producing it exactly as it is.

Then a lot of very intelligent people, who are mostly businessmen, are going to say, "I've been off on this track, I've been totally involved elsewhere and now I'm seeing the consequences of that. I'm going to put my energy somewhere else."

There is something else available. There are going to be more luminous beings, there are going to be more people who work in purity and in love, who are not fighting and not manipulating. People are going to start to reach that place in themselves and they are going to say, "Let's work together. We could make this deal this way, but if we do, I make some money, but you lose some money. Maybe there is a way where we can both work together."

Then there is going to be a harmony within ourselves. As we stop fighting inside, we'll become accepting of ourselves. As we become accepting of ourselves, a love grows. As the acceptance happens here, it happens there. If I accept this, I start to accept that. If I love this, I start to love that. If I support this, I start to support that, because in a way anything I do is not in isolation. If you upset somebody somewhere, those waves are affecting you. If you care for somebody somewhere, those waves are affecting you and you start to reach a very beautiful place in yourself.

Then if you want to play business, you can play business. If you want to be an artist, you can be an artist. If you live your truth, whereever you are, whatever you're doing, then this beautiful contentment comes. There is no work. There is just being. There is just allowing. There is just enjoying.

Roxi: You talked about businessmen possibly becoming the new world leaders. It does seem that the present leaders, the politicians and the religious leaders, have failed. I'm wondering, if businessmen do become the new world leaders if they will fail as well.

Paul: What I was looking at was everyone becoming their own leader. We'll have people who are doing certain functions, but eventually there will be no leaders. There will be people who have reached a certain level of consciousness in themselves and they will be an encouragement to others. To be in the presence of their vibrations will be very uplifting. My feeling is a really intelligent person would not be a politician. They might want to be but wouldn't because of the conditions that are involved and the frustration of the lack of power. A successful business person is usually total in what he is doing. He puts his whole being to something and goes there and then makes it work.

When dimensions start to change and the whole world starts to change it's way of being, these may be the first people to wake up and say, "This isn't working, something new is supposed to happen. What is it?" Then they may bring that energy to expanding their own consciousness and discovering who they are, but not in the restricted way they used to. It needs totality, but you can't do it. You have to be it. Then these people will be one of the first groups to awaken.

Roxi: When you talk about totality, I'm not always sure what you mean. I've found that totality has meant an exclusion of other things. I'm wondering how a businessman, if he is really total, can also include a happy family life and have time with his friends.

Paul: I'm talking about a totality that includes. So when somebody wakes up to the fact that what he is doing is not working, and he needs to find out who he is and he wants to become fully conscious of himself, he becomes total in that. But it includes everything. It includes the wife, the husband, the children, the work. It includes, it does not exclude. But it keeps the focus on the most important thing. There is one more thing about that. To attain the ultimate that is available on this planet, you need this totality. You need this total focus, and along the way you will become aware that you can't go there if you are holding anything. When I say holding it, I don't mean having it, I mean holding it. So, you can have your money, your family and your possessions, but if you hold them, you contract. To know who you are, you have to expand and expand. You have to let go and let go.

Many of the most successful businessmen do not attain their success technically. They might know the market, they might know their subject completely, but their decisions do not come from that place. Their decisions come from intuition, and that is accessed through openness and letting go. You do the groundwork, you get the figures and then you let go into another place that expands and includes.

What the person doesn't know is that they are seeing what is called the future. In fact, it is not the future at all. It's the present being lived on a different level. They know the state of the market in what we call the future, because they have let go. Now, they don't register this cognitively, but they have seen something, they have had a flash of something. They make a decision and they don't even know why they have made it. It's come from the intuition. The intuition is accessed by letting go, by expanding.

Roxi: It seems to me that's the hardest thing of all, spending ten, twenty years, maybe longer, creating a fortune and then letting go of it. I understand what you are saying, that it doesn't mean you have to give it all away, but this attitude of letting go is hard to grasp.

I'm remembering a quote from Jesus. "It's easier for a camel to pass through the eye of the needle than for a rich man to enter the gates of Heaven." It seems that it has always been difficult for rich and successful people to really experience this letting go.

Paul: We have interpreted that as you can't enter the Kingdom of Heaven if you have riches, so therefore you have to be poor. "Blessed are the poor, blessed are the meek." Then the rich man doesn't want to do that, he doesn't want to live like that. As I was saying, the truth isn't either way, it's right in the middle. In one way it's easier to give away your riches, because to have them and not possess them, or not be possessed by them, is very difficult. So some people say, "This isn't working so I'll give it away." Nothing is changed, the same seed is still there, the same attitude is there.

It's disconnecting and living consciously with that wealth, living beautifully with it. Poverty, dirt, ugliness they are all ridiculous. Nobody needs that.

Roxi: When I read the financial papers, the general feeling from the experts is still one of gloom, maybe with touches of optimism, but the overall feeling is uncertainty. It does seem that the financial recession that we had on the stock exchange last autumn will recur sometime. There is a general shakiness about the money markets around the world. Is there a bright side to this?

Paul: The bright side is not what most people would see as the bright side. As everybody knows now, with all this information on the subject, the whole financial system is based on myth. It's all an agreement, it doesn't actually exist. Money doesn't mean anything unless everybody agrees that it does. Gold is worthless unless somebody wants it or it means something to him. It's all a fantasy, and it's built up, and it's got to this point that is very shaky. It was supposed to do that, and it is supposed to collapse. It's meant to happen so that we can wake up. What's been happening is that we have all been saying, "When I have this wealth, when I have these possessions, then I'll be alright." The people who have this wealth and these possessions find that it is not alright. So they go to drugs or sex or alcohol or something to avoid this point, or commit suicide in some way because it doesn't work. We have come to a point on this planet where there isn't time for five billion people to realize that. What we are going to do through our higher Selves, our future Selves, is create this collapse and through this we are going to wake up. Everybody is going to wake up, this is nothing new. The Book of the

Revelations said, "And they shall eat their children. The poverty will be so much, there will be nothing." The whole system will collapse and then people have to wake up to another reality.

Another reality is that, not only finance is an illusion but this whole dimension is an illusion. It's something we create. Generally people think that we are now flying in airplanes because we discovered the technology. It's not that. Somebody wanted to fly, wanted to fly so much, he found a way to fly. Somebody wanted to go faster, he created a way to go faster. We are creating this reality. We are creating the pollution, we are creating the wars, we are creating the violence. We can create abundance and we can create beauty. If we want it enough, it'll happen.

At the moment we are not wanting it enough, so other forces, other dimensions, which are us in another form, are going to remove this illusion and say, "Let's start again."

Roxi: What's the next step for businessmen, businesswomen, who maybe don't know very much about meditation or spiritual matters, but they know there is something more in their lives? They have their material success, maybe they have their families who are happy. What is their next step?

Paul: There isn't a next step unless the person wants it. It's no good believing anybody or saying, "That's a good idea." You have to want it. It's like if you want to give up smoking. It's no good just reading the Surgeon General's warning on the packet, that's too remote. One day, if you realize what you are doing to your system, if you can feel it in your body, you have this realization in yourself, and you want to stop smoking. At that moment you have just stopped, right then. Your body goes through its withdrawals, everything does its craving, but you have stopped and you are never going to go back, because you have had that realization. If you don't, then it's a good idea and you'll maybe attempt it and you'll sit and do your meditation every now and again, but you won't stay with it. What usually takes people to that point is that they reached the peak and there is nothing further to gain. Or they have a near–death experience or they have a financial collapse or somebody close to them dies. Something shakes them and says, "Look at your life."

If you start to wake up, if you just start to use this intelligence that has taken you to financial success and success in many other ways, to start to inquire, you start to get interested, because waking up is the greatest challenge. The challenge on the outside is nothing, the challenge on the inside is incredible.

Who had that thought?

Where did that thought come from?

Who had that emotion?

Where did that anger come from?

Where did that energy came from that just took you over and got you angry?

Who is this?

This is the greatest adventure. So, the first thing is, you've got to really want it. If you do, then you can start to read some books, you can start to talk to people, mention how you feel.

When you want it, you'll get it. So you quoted Jesus earlier, he is also quoted as saying, "Knock and it will be open, seek and you will find." As soon as you say, "What's the next step?" it's presented to you.

It may not be presented in a form that is convenient to you! Then you might say, "No thank you I'll stay here." It may say, "No, you need to let that job go. You need to move, you need to let go of that family, you are not happy there, they are not happy with you."

As soon as you want the truth, the truth is made available, because it's always there. It's just that you don't see it, because it's not convenient. So, the first thing is to want it. As soon as you want it, the next level is revealed to you. Are you ready? If you are ready, then the next level appears, and the next.

Then you may have heard of somebody who has been away on a course, something like this one, and has transformed. You see her when she comes back and you can tell that she is not the same person. You ask her what happened. And she says, "Well,I put by six months of my life or six weeks of my life or a part of my life to really explore myself." Then, do you have the courage to do that, to go to a place where you are really going to have a chance to look at your life?

If you had just bought a new computer for your business, then you would probably send one of your employees on a course so that they could learn how to work it properly. You would send him to an expert, because the expert can teach him in the quickest time.

So, if you want to attain something, you would say, who has something to share? I'm not talking about going to a guru, somebody to whom you give your power away. I consider that ugly. What I'm talking about is going to an expert. For instance, if you wanted to learn carpentry, you would go to a master carpenter. If you wanted to play the guitar, you'd go to somebody who plays the guitar well. You'd go and watch him and sense him.

In this game, something happens a little more than with a carpenter or a computer teacher or a guitar player. What happens is, as you reveal something to yourself, a higher vibration starts to happen. The whole system starts to work in a different way. When somebody comes close to that who is receptive, he starts to feel that and it vibrates his system in a similar way, he starts to catch something. It reminds him of something. However, nothing transfers.

It has been said that something transfers from the master to the pupil. It's not true, nothing transfers. All that happens is that, as this is working at a certain vibration, when you come close to it, your vibration will start to work in harmony. So as soon as you want it enough, you start to see where you need to go and what you need to do. Then eventually, just out of your awareness and common sense, you'll start to spend some time each day just sitting and saying, "Who is this? What is this? What's going on?" To do that you may need to disconnect from the outside.

One of the best ways of doing that is just sitting with closed eyes or looking down in front of you with half–closed eyes. One of the dangers of closing the eyes is that the mind comes up and spins the fantasies. Some people find it easier with eyes half–closed, just looking in front of them, not being in and not being out. Then there is nothing to do, but to watch. No mantras, no magic formulas, just watch the process and don't get attached. It's easy, until along comes this thought that you didn't tell so and so to do this and if they don't do it they might miss the stock market or this might happen. And then your mind is there and then you are lost. Watch. Even if you lose money, just watch. Just watch these things go past, they are all there, the mind is still as active as ever, maybe more active than before.

But you don't get caught in any of the frames, the pictures within you, you just keep watching. As you keep watching, you'll find the mind continues but you're getting further and further away from the picture. Eventually it is like somebody else's picture, somebody else's mind. Then you start to slow down and a stillness starts to happen and you find you are detached. With that detachment comes a peace and then it becomes easier to do it each time. Then eventually when you open your eyes, you'll find the mind is not so strong, you'll find that your habits are not so in control. You're not so possessed anymore because you have found this place that can watch. Quietness and stillness starts to be a part of your life.

Somebody gets upset, something happens and you have this still place that watches. Sometimes the mind and the body and the emotions will get just as upset as they usually do, but you've found this place of watching and then...again Jesus called it the peace that passes all understanding.

Roxi: One of the things that I found, especially after I first started coming here, was that when I went back to London and had business meetings, my attitude often reflected how the meeting went. I was mainly dealing with musicians, and often historically I may have had meetings with them which had been problematical.

If I went into the meeting with the attitude that there would be a problem, there may be a problem, but if I went in with the attitude that, "Well, there was a problem last time but this time I don't know what's going to happen." It gave a space for something new. On the outside it seems that if you create space for something different, you lose time. But in a way, I've found the opposite to be true. If I created space, things still got done and I had more time.

Paul: This can be talked about on many levels, because there are many running simultaneously. Let's talk about one level. A trained racing car driver who's trained himself with experience up to the fastest Formula One cars is working at a different time vibration and a different space vibration than you are. If you are driving along a road and somebody enters your lane and is coming straight at you, your system isn't trained to handle that. It will probably go into a panic. When it goes into a panic, it loses time and it loses space.

Literally, you have less time and less space than a trained driver. A racing driver will not panic because he's had life and death situations many times. What he will do is look at the speed of the car, look at the space, look at what's right and left and where to go and he'll have a hundred times more space and time than you because you've gone into a panic. Now he actually has more time and more space. He's more likely to go through a gap that you wouldn't even try because you're in a panic. He would say, "I can get through there," and calmly do it. His whole system will shake afterwards. He'll be just as frightened as you were, but the thing is he's trained and he has more time and space, literally, in a way the mind doesn't understand. That's one level.

Another level is this: when you walk into the board room, you are vibrating at a different level. You have decided that you're not going to be worried about any disturbance. When you come in, you come in with another vibration. Snake charms do work if the native has faith in the medicine man. When the snake charm is put on, the native says, "Now I'm safe from snakes." A snake comes and he thinks this snake can't bite him, so he doesn't panic. When he doesn't panic, he doesn't change his vibration. He doesn't give off the odor of fear to which the snake is likely to react. If you've reached that place of calmness, that place of gentleness, it's vibrating around you. It's glowing around you whether people can see it or not. Then they move in harmony to that.

Then there is a third level and this is an abstract level and one that the mind can't understand because it can't be understood. We create our own reality. Another way of putting that is, in each moment there is no time and there is no space. Everything is happening now. Not only is everything happening now, but every possibility of now is happening now.

One possibility is that you're going to walk into that board room and your musicians are going to make trouble. Another possibility is that you are going to walk into that board room and they are not going to create trouble. A third possibility is that you walk in and you see luminous beings. You make the choice, you choose the level to which you move. What influences your choice is your conditioning, what you have been told is possible.

At one time, nobody ran a mile in four minutes because it was impossible. Then Roger Bannister did it. It became possible so other people did it. There were no diet changes no extra training, just that somebody else did it. In one race they didn't run the four–minute mile, in the next race they did. They chose a different reality. The mind can't understand this, but all this is an illusion that we create, moment to moment. We create it, we let it go. We create it, it fades away. You can create what you want to create.

Roxi: When I look at this with my mind, it just scrambles and I can make no sense of it, but the key for me is the word impossible. I know that in business, in my own way, I've done things which I previously thought were impossible. I think that's what happens in business to a lot of people who are successful. They do things that everybody else feels are impossible. They may even logically feel it themselves but they still go for it, keep open and see what happens.

Paul: If you are not identified with it happening, in other words, if it doesn't have to happen, you go in with a loose vibration. If it has to happen, then you are making things difficult because often that tension creates the opposite. If it's a sort of open gamble, a conscious gamble, "This might not pay off, but I want to play this game. I want to see." There is a possibility. Somewhere even in this impossibility, something tells you to do it anyway. You go in with this attitude, you will create your own reality.

Roxi: What is the secret of your success?

Paul: Again we can talk about it on many different levels. One level is that I have always been basically an innocent person, although I haven't been innocent all the time. There is an inquiry about me, about everything. I want to know, but I want to know from a place of not knowing, not from a place of knowing. So the first thing is I don't know.

The second thing is that I was born with an integrity. Basically, I don't cheat, I don't manipulate and I'm a straight person. So I haven't had to pay for things that I've built up around me, because you have to pay for everything. Everything you unbalance has to balance. The next thing is, I'm finished with things very quickly. If I go into something, I go into something with such totality, it fulfills itself. I get to know all I need to know, there is nothing left unfinished.

That's what happened for me with money. One of the things that happened for me was I built up a certain amount of money and then I got a reputation, so I had a future. I got a family, I got everything I wanted and something still wasn't fulfilled.

Then what came to me was the message, that you're not going to find out while you've got money. Now I'm not saying that's everybody's message. That was my message. I wanted to know what it was like to be without any money. So one day in India, I gave away all my money. I emptied my pockets and I stood there in the middle of Bombay with no money and no support and not knowing anybody, just to find out what would happen. I wanted to know what would happen if I did that. I gave the money to my wife and my children so they could take care of themselves and they went away and that left just me and a spiritual teacher and a few people around. Basically I had nothing, because the spiritual teacher didn't have any money either. Nothing. So there I was in Bombay with nothing, living on bananas eventually, and from that I built up again.

I built that up from my consciousness instead of my unconsciousness, or what other people told me. Then I found that by letting go, everything comes. But you never know that until you've done it. You'll never know whether your partner loves you or not, until you let him or her go. You even encourage them to leave you if they are attracted to somebody else. And if they come back to you, if they spend that night with you, you know that this person really wants to be with you that night. You let your money go, you just stop holding, you stop hoarding, you stop all that tension around it. If it stays, it's supposed to stay. If you have to hold it, you're burning yourself out to hold it and that burning will kill you, because you are spending energy that has to be repaid. You usually repay it in cancer or a heart attack or some other illness.

If you dare to let go, what remains is what is meant to remain. There really isn't a way around that. You see, I didn't give the money away, there was no wrench to it. It was, "This money needs to go. I need to be in this state." I didn't do anything. There was no sacrifice, there was no suffering. It was just like a great adventure. It was like somebody was saying, "I'm going to climb this rock with all my ropes and my rings and my hammers and my ice picks," and somebody else says, "I'm going to see if I can get up there with no ropes, just a pair of nice shoes, a little bit of training and see if I can get up there with no help. Nobody pulling me up, no safety nets below." It's an adventure.

Roxi: It's a gamble. That's what I like about it. It's why I like to be with you when you talk, because I feel the excitement that you have and you've had living in the unknown and gambling. If I again bring that back to me, I see that I gamble and there is more. It's not to do with recklessness. Uusually gambling is connected with being reckless. It isn't that. It's to do with my heart, am I willing to expose myself more and more and more? Because if I do, it is the unknown and I could lose, yet it could open up something I didn't know about.

Paul: That's what I've done, over and over again. It used to be in a cycle of two years and three months, and then when I was in this spiritual commune, it was thirteen years of total devotion to that. We are doing the same here, two years and three months. We are in one of the most beautiful places in the world. We are living in absolute luxury. People are coming from all over the world to be with us. Everything is set and fine and, in a few days time, we give it all up. We have a stepping stone, which is the six–week project, and then, nothing. Out of that nothing the ultimate can happen.

If we hold onto this and modify it, we'll keep our base and modify that but it will restrict our possibilities. Now, maybe we'll crash, but I've never crashed yet. Every time I've let go, it's been better. Every woman whom I've let go of, or who's let go of me, the next one has been more fulfilling. Every situation has grown, everything in every way. If I give something away, something more beautiful comes. It's just this system has a built–in program to survive and that means hold. It keeps you restricted to being mediocre.

Let go and let go, and just make space.

CHAPTER NINE

CREATIVITY

An Interview by Roxi McNay

Roxi: The idea of this video is as a trailer for a new TV series based on creativity, and I realize already that I have an expectation of what I would like this video to be. I want it to be really good so the producer of the program is very impressed and wants to fly you over to new York for the TV program. I can see I am already a bit out of my center! If I come back I see that the subject does interest me. I find that creativity can be neurotic much of the time. Many painters and musicians have used their creativity to release neuroses and I have found that I have got something out of their release as well as they. I am just now thinking of painters. Constable comes to mind as an example of someone who painted very beautiful country scenes which are very peaceful to look at, and people like Picasso or Salvador Dali created far more erratic pictures which are very neurotic and cathartic on the face of it. Do you have anything to say about this connection?

Paul: The first thing to talk about is your presence here in this moment. If you look at the way you are sitting and the way you are talking, it's because it has to do with the future and not now. We are making a video, it may go to New York, and we are here and now. If we make this connection with our hearts, in this presence, in the present, that presence may come over on the video. If we are not here, nothing is here. It's just more pollution of ideas on the planet and we have enough ideas that don't work. There is nothing wrong with the ideas themselves, it's just that nobody was there when they were expressed. If somebody is there, you will see it when he is painting, you will hear it when he is playing music. You will see it when he does a sculpture. You will know when a person is present. If you go to the Taj Mahal, you know that that designer was present. If you go to many of the beautiful buildings and cathedrals around Europe, you will know that those designers were present. That was usually because they were religious people, religious in the real sense, not in the false sense which is nearly always the case now. In fact, most of these people were sufis, even the ones who designed the Christian Cathedrals. They were of an order called the Naqshbandi, which means designers. They designed many of the beautiful gardens, and many of the famous statues and buildings. Their ideas came from being in the present, from being in the now. The present and the now are always perfect. You can feel it when it is happening. Lets go back to creativity.

Everybody is wonderfully, magnificently creative. We were born creative, we were born with a light, with a spark, with a glory of creativity, every single being. Then it gets covered.

With some people, it was a little covered when they were born. It was there but it was covered from previous lives or karma. We are born and then it gets covered over.

We are told, "This is the way you paint. This is the way you make music. This is the way you present yourself." All these ideas were from people who were not creative. They were dead, they were repeating dead things that came from dead people. Wonderful creativity is burning in each person, and for that creativity to glow, to shine, the layers of conditioning need to be let go of. You need to let go of what you have been told, your ideas and theories. Let everything go until you don't know anything, then you are creative. Being in the not knowing is the most creative, because you are here.

If I assume you are a man, if I assume you are of a certain age and a certain background, then I assume your name and I assume your friendship. I am not seeing you at all. I am just seeing all these layers. If I didn't do that, then we are just togetherness and if we stay with that togetherness, there is no togetherness, because there is only one. There is no two thinkings separating, there is just one togetherness. Then anything you say and anything I say will be creative, because it will come from a place of not knowing.

Let's go back to what you were saying about people catharting their neuroses. That's true, but what else can they do, because they are not in touch with their creativity? They are not in touch with that clear place in themselves. Occasionally it happens that someone does reach that place. You can go through an art gallery, you can walk through hall after hall and suddenly there is one. Then you know that at the moment when that person painted that painting, he was in his creativity, he was in his light, he was in his pureness. You can see others that impress you, because that light is shining, but it shines through the levels of neurosis. Then there are other paintings that are nothing but neuroses, just somebody who is so upset and disturbed inside that he threw it on to the canvas or he threw it into music or a piece of sculpture. It is disturbing because this person is putting his distorted consciousness out, and it affects you.

If somebody who has reached clarity and lives in that place makes some sounds that we call music or puts something on to a canvas that we call a picture, when you look at it, his vibrations will connect with your vibrations. For a moment you will feel some stillness or some joy. You will feel the place where that particular piece of creativity came from. You will feel the silence. You are right, most people cathart onto the canvas or into the music and it is good for them, it helps them get rid of it. If they keep it inside, they will either explode, or they will get ill with it, or something will happen. But it is very destructive for the people who are listening, because they have already got neuroses of their own, without picking up somebodys else's. You say somewhere it satisfies you. Yes it is like an addiction, you get drawn to it. If you are feeling violent, you are more likely to turn on a boxing program to increase that violence. If you start to become still and quiet, if you find a way of doing that, then you will start to get drawn to healing things, not other people's catharsis. You start to get pulled to things, either music or visual things or something around you that helps you enter that peaceful state.

Roxi: I haven't played any music for a long time. Sometimes when I go out and I hear music playing on the radio, even if it is playing softly, the force with which it comes out surprises me. I am now thinking of England where the main radio station is called Radio One. Basically, they play the same music all day long, usually dance music with happy lyrics, and I see that it is a kind of fantasy world most people live in. They turn on the radio, they hear a happy song and it raises them to a happier level. On the face of it it seems good, but then I think it is probably like taking a valium and just suppresses their feelings.

Paul: The trouble is, it is over the top of their distress, and the distress eventually causes some sort of illness or unpleasantness in their lives. When you are talking about different types of music, there are many, many levels of consciousness on this planet. The majority of people are actually asleep. They are living automatically, they are acting like machines. If something happens, they react in a certain way. They are sheep and they are asleep. They choose their lives, nothing is making them do it. A few people start to wake up a little bit, and then there is another level to that, and then another. Then there is a big jump to another level, where you really wake up.

When you wake up, you suddenly see how asleep everybody is and you feel alien to them, because you are alien. If you listen to the different levels of music from the violent catharsis of some rock music, up through to the pleasant classical, out through jazz and into the classical Eastern and Western, if you keep listening with tremendous awareness, you will stop listening to music. The reason is that each piece of music will pull you down, even the best classical music, because it is not quite right for you. At a certain stage you can feel you are being pulled up. Certain music can pull you up. It has a certain vibration and often it was created by people who were awake at that time, and it conveys the feeling of that awakeness to you. But if you keep going you will find that you have surpassed their level of consciousness and then when you play it, you will come down. When some people take psychedelic drugs, they come down because they live in a state that is higher than the drug. If you are totally looking for consciousness, if that is your whole life, then very soon you will reach this level where almost anything that affects you brings you down. You are living in a higher state that most people are afraid of. When you are there, even if you don't say anything, you are creative. You are creative the way you stand, the way you sleep, the way you move. Everything you say is creative because it does not come from a place of neurosis, a place of knowledge. It comes from a place of not knowing. It just flows out, and then music pulls you down. If you want music at this stage, you can close your eyes and you will find there is music there.

Do you want to try it?

Just close your eyes. There is the humming of the recording equipment, the singing of birds, and then inside you, there is a chorus. It's not like music as such; it is sounds and vibrations, a humming or a singing. If you include all of that, it is a wonderful vibration, if you just let go into it...

You better come back now.

Roxi: As I come out of that space, I feel even more aware of my voice. The humming of the machine too, has more of a fineness about it. I am looking at why I don't stay there. It requires incredible courage to stay in this space because there are so many distractions, so many energies that are capable of pulling me out unless I stay totally in my own clarity. There is always something or somebody trying to distract me.

Paul: Again, if you want it enough, you will do it. If anything else is more important you will be distracted. There is a wonderful story about a man who was a very good archer in his village. He was the best archer. He was so much better than anyone else that he was considered a genius.

One day he said to himself, "I would like to be the world's greatest archer, not just better than anyone in my village, but the greatest." He was talking to a friend about this and the friend said, "Oh the world's greatest archer lives not far from here." So, he goes to find him and tells him what he wants. The world's greatest archer says to him, "I can help you. First of all, you must go back and do this exercise." The exercise was, he had to sit in a chair and watch an insect on the window in a spider's web, and do nothing else but watch it. It took him months and months and the archer didn't tell him why he was doing it. One day, suddenly he could see the insect on the spider's web as though it was right in front of his eyes. He could see every detail, every scale, every hair. Suddenly he had a new vision and he said, "This is what he wanted me to see." He goes dashing back and he says, "It has happened." The world's greatest archer says, "Good!"

Then he gave him another exercise. This was to lie under his wife's weaving machine, and watch the shuttle fly backwards and forwards. He was there for months and months and months, and then one day it was as though the shuttle was going slowly, although he knew it wasn't. He knew he had reached a new place of space and time and he rushed back and told the archer. And so it goes on, month after month until a new level of consciousness happened in the archer.

That was because nothing else was more important in his life. He also had a wife who was happy to support him doing this! Something happened to that man because he was prepared to put that much energy into it. You are being drawn out all the time by your addictions, by your habits. They keep trying to pull you out and five billion people are trying to draw you out too. They don't want you to be special. They don't want you to attain something. If you do, you are going to show them that they could do that as well, and they are too lazy. It means giving up things, it means letting go of things. If you want it, it will start to happen. The only place it happens is right here and right now.

When you came back, you could hear everything more clearly because you had slowed down, you had forgotten the camera, you had forgotten we were making a video, you had forgotten the future and the past. You weren't in the past and you weren't in the future. You just went into that exercise and you were here. When you are here and you focus on that machine, you will find that it is not just one hum. There are levels and levels of vibration in there. If you were to listen to the birds, you would find that there are hundreds of birds all singing their different songs in different ways. If you were to go inside yourself, you would find that there is not just one song. There are levels and levels of sound inside there, all different vibrations of consciousness. But to be in touch with those things you need to be here and now, to slow down and be prepared to be different.

Nobody's different. Everybody is the same but nobody realizes it. However, everybody has a uniqueness, everybody has a flavor of his own, but at the same time we have the same vibration running through all of us. When you wake up, you become aware that people are asleep and then you start to feel alone. If you stay with that, you will find in each person that you can get in touch with the vibration which is the same as yours.

Then you are not alone. In one way you are, in another way you are one with everything. But it takes courage, because suddenly you will feel like an alien on the planet, and wonder what you are doing among all these sleepwalkers. You are here to wake up. When you wake up, you are here to help other people wake up, if that is what they want.

Roxi: Most people are creative in an area. It may be art, making money, music or fashion, and they have a reputation which is built on success. I can see that you know your truth, and success in other people's eyes is of no importance whatsoever. I can sense the tremendous sense of freedom you must feel with that.

Paul: When you find yourself you are free, and then there is nothing to prove because you know. If you want to be creative from that place, you can be creative in any way you want. Different people do have different flavors, and sometimes a person has been a great musician in past lives, and so when they become creative that is what they want to play with. Somebody else may have been a great painter. Somebody else may have just talked well or been a gardener, or an architect or just a cleaner. It does not make any difference. When you have found yourself, you are creative in whatever you do.

I'll tell you another story. It's about a famous king a long time ago and his hobby was music. Wherever there was a great musician, he would engage that musician to live in his court. So people from all around used to come to the concerts that his musicians gave. He had among his musicians the finest singer that anyone had ever heard. He was a young man and a wonderful singer. The king was being creative one day and looking around and saying, "Well I wonder if there is anybody better than he?" Then he thought if there is somebody better than he, it would be his teacher. So he calls the singer and says, "Did you have a teacher and if so was he better than you?" The singer replied, "Incomparable." The king said, " Why isn't he here?" The singer explained that he wouldn't come. "I will order him," answered the king.

Again the singer explained that even if the king did order him to come he wouldn't sing. However, he also offered, "If you want to hear him, I can arrange it, but you will have to do exactly what I say." The king agreed. The condition was that the king must dress like a merchant.

They went out on the streets so that no one recognized them. They journeyed for a long time and towards the evening came to some woods. The musician told the king that they had to stay in the woods all night. So they stayed, and as dawn came up they looked down and a little way away was a river and a tiny little wooden hut. Out of that hut came the most wonderful singing that the king had ever heard. The king was absolutely enraptured, he was in a state of meditation. The singing went on and on and the king disappeared into it. When the singing had stopped, the musician took the king quietly away and after a long, long time the King came back to his normal consciousness and said, "I have never heard anything like it. I have never dreamt anything like it. One thing puzzles me, though. Your voice is as good as that, the timbre is as good, the sound is like that, yet it is not like that. Why is that so?" And the musician replied, "Because I sing for you."

If you sing for anything, if you do anything for anything, it is contaminated. It is not just from your being, it is not just from your light, from the joy of your expression, it's for something. In that way it is contaminated. It means that it is not enough unto itself because you are not enough unto yourself. As soon as you become enough unto yourself, it means that you have accepted yourself, you realize yourself, you love yourself. You will love everything you do and if other people love it, that is wonderful. If not, it is the same.

Roxi: It sounds so simple.

Paul: It is very simple but it is not easy. It is not easy because you are bombarded with conditioning and this conditioning will control you while you are unconscious. If you are conscious, if you are present, if you are in this moment you don't have to deal with your conditioning, it will fade.

If you go to sleep, you become a machine again. You can become a painting machine, a music machine, an architectural machine. You are a machine because then you are working on your programming. If you come here in this moment, totally present, all your training is available just as a tool, but you are coming from your essence.

If you are really coming from your essence, the essence of your essence, you are coming from the essence of the universe because at that place there is only One. At that place, everything is connected. Everything flows. You are the creator.

1. Lady Chohan. *Chohan was a core member of I.A.M. and The Six Month Project. She is the interviewer in Chapters 2,3,4 and 14.*

2. Paul Lowe *in 1987.*

3. Velusia Van Horssen. *Velusia and Paul were together on many of Paul's world tours. She was a founding member of I.A.M., a core member of the Six Month Project and the interviewer in chapter 17.*

4. Phoenicia Graham and Martin Gerrish. *Phoenicia was a core member of I.A.M. and they were both core members of the Six Month Project. Phoenicia is the interviewer in chapter 16.*

5. Clare Patricia Soloway. *Clare and Paul were together on many adventures including marriage and two children, Tania and Ryan. Clare is the interviewer in chapter 6.*

6. Paul Lowe *in 1984.*

7. Salila. *Interviewer in chapter 18 and core member of Six Month Project.*

8. *Villa Volpi on the shores of Lago Maggoire on the Italian side of the Swiss/Italian border, which was the home of I.A.M. and The Six Month Project. Most of the interviews were done here.*

9. *The last day of the Six Month Project–28th February 1988.*

10. Roxi McNay. *This book was conceived, edited and produced by him. He is the interviewer in chapters 1,8 and 9. A core member during the Six Month Project, he is at present nurturing the practical side of Paul's work.*

11. Don Pachuta M.D. *Interviewer in chapter 12 and author of "The Life You Save May Be Your Own." Don is a physician practising in the Baltimore/Washington area, with a speciality in infectious diseases.*

12. Paul Lowe and Kyala Zacharias. *November 1988. Kyala was a core member during the Six Month Project and has been Paul's companion since summer 1987.*

CHAPTER TEN

BEYOND SUCCESS

An Interview by Teresa Bassels

Teresa: I wanted to do this interview so I could show it to some of my friends who work at the Common Market in Brussels. I have been talking and sharing with them over the past years and have the feeling that it is very important that they hear what you have to say.

When I look at them, I can see that they have their material lives well together. They are successful. They have very beautiful houses, and yet they have a lack of motivation in life. It's something like general dissatisfaction or frustration.

Paul: This is a very good place to be, and it's also an extremely dangerous place. When we are born onto this plane, onto this planet, we have a system in here for survival and it strives for that. So, it strives to get good grades, to find a good job, to have a good family, to take care of itself. And most people's energy is spent on just that all their lives. They never get what they want, they just think they are on this planet to survive, to get things right. What is happening now is that more and more people are seeing that when they have achieved what they wanted in their lives, it doesn't work. It does not work because it is not supposed to work. That isn't what we came to this planet for. It's what this system does, it has to survive. Of course, you have to take care of the body, you have to protect yourself and your family, but that isn't what we came here for. We came to this planet for something much bigger than that.

The seed that is in us that wants to survive is very tiny compared with another energy that is striving to remember. This other energy wants to remember where it came from and where it's going to. It wants to remember what this whole thing is about, what it is for. Unfortunately, although this seed is much bigger, it's feminine, it's passive, it's gentle, it has no aggression. This other survival seed is very small, but it pushes and is aggressive, and so this other bigger seed just lies there, mostly dormant. Then the religions come along and say, "We'll take care of that, you give us some money, come on Sundays and everything will be okay." And it is not okay. It does not work.

It does not work because this seed says, "I want everything. I want your total attention and if you do not give me that, you will never be happy." It is saying you are not going to be happy, not because it doesn't love you, but because it does love you. It is not going to let you be happy until you realize what you came to this dimension for, so it puts things in the way. Your life is going along very nicely. You have everything you want and suddenly it gives you an illness, or a car accident, or you lose a beloved and it says, "Wake up!" This dimension is not about survival, it is about something far greater. It is about the things that the Christs have come for, the Buddhas have come to tell you. There is something much, much more available on this dimension, on this planet. Once you realize that and you become available, you will never be frustrated again. You will never be bored again. You will never again wonder what you are here for, because you will see that remembering who you are is such a great adventure.

There are levels and levels and levels. When a person attains materially what they want, then in one way it is a very beautiful place because they can now start to look where they need to look. Unfortunately, they usually don't, so they get into this frustrating and stuck place.

Teresa: I understand that very well, and I can see that they are in a position to start looking at that. Can you suggest how they can become aware of it?

Paul: There are a few things here. First of all, there is not much encouragement to look because most of what religion offers isn't fulfilling. I mean by this the orthodox churches, the eastern churches and the gurus. The new age doesn't offer anything for a sophisticated person either. It's either materialism or spiritualism and both of them are bullshit. There is something else that is real. When Christ came and had a message, and it was a very beautiful message, it was a message for two thousand years ago, to the level of consciousness two thousand years ago. Since then, it has been corrupted and corrupted. Exactly the same thing happened with Buddha, a beautiful message that has since been corrupted and is no longer appropriate anyway. What is needed now is something totally different and this has come to the planet.

That is what we are doing here, and that's what some other movements are doing, something for the intelligent person that doesn't say just believe this and you will be all right, because that is very degrading. This new movement is saying, "Don't believe anything. Don't take anything for granted. Start to look for yourself. We have discovered things, so we can share those with you and maybe we can give you some guidance on your way, but you have to do it. Going to church on Sunday won't do it, sitting down for ten minutes a day won't do it. It is going to take something more." You ask how they are going to look. Possibly one day they might see someone on their television and feel that that person is seeing something they are not, and they say, "I want to meet him."

Another way is that they might have what is termed a spiritual experience, either in their dreams, or when they are walking in the country one day. Actually, there is nothing spiritual about it. What happens is their eyes open to other dimensions that are here now. Millions of people are having these experiences on the planet, especially now, but they don't tell anybody because they think they are going crazy. They think there is something wrong because that is what the psychologists have told them. They have been told, "You are hallucinating. It's because you took drugs. You are under stress." So they might have a spiritual experience, hear that somebody else has had this experience and say, "I want to know more about this."

Also, they may be so complete that they are just bored, and then they start to look.

A less pleasant way is that they have an illness or their beloved has an illness. We often get subtle messages and if we don't hear the messages, they get less subtle. So a person might have a very serious illness and then have what is called a near–death experience. This means he almost dies and in this place of let go, when he has stopped holding things together, sees the other dimensions. People experience them so strongly and so powerfully that they can't deny them. Then when they come back they say, "That wasn't a hallucination, that was more real than this is, I want to know how I can live in that level."

The most unpleasant way is what is happening to this planet at the moment. In its present form it is winding down. All the things we have are starting to disappear. Now at the moment it's just a rumble, but it's going to shake the whole planet to such a degree that nobody will be able to ignore it. What we are hearing about AIDS is probably a tiny fraction of what that disease is ultimately going to do to the planet. The incidence of cancer is likely to increase dramatically. The effects of radiation will probably be much more than we realize. Pollution, the hole in the ozone, the financial situation, this planet is going to come to such a place of insecurity that there will be nowhere to turn. There will be no security. Nothing will be able to be taken for granted.

People are going to say, "What's going on, where can I turn?" Then they are going to look. Jesus is quoted as saying something like, "Look and you will find, knock and you will be heard." It's true. When you want it, it is available. So the people to whom you are taking this interview are the people who have started to look. Now the people who really wanted to look have come here. They are part of this program. Anybody can be here, and anybody can be part of this program if they want to, and that is the key to awakening. The key is wanting it enough. If your survival or your job or your family is more important, then you won't find your freedom.

I am not saying that you don't have your money, your job, your family. You can have everything. Again, Jesus said, "Seek ye first the kingdom of God, and everything else is added on to you." You can have everything, but your priority must be to wake up and know who you are. If you want that enough, then it starts to happen. The books you need to read will turn up, the TV programs will come on when you are ready to see them. You will hear about where you need to go, and the people you need to meet. As soon as you want it, it starts to happen for you. So you ask how people are going to start to look, very soon we are all going to have to start looking.

A lot of people think that something is being done to them by this. That is not true. In a way that most people don't understand, there are levels and levels of consciousness, and we exist on all of them at the same time. This planet has to change. To change in the ways that we have been looking at in the past is impossible. It doesn't work. Everybody is saying that somebody else should do it. Somebody else should stop the pollution, somebody else should stop the wars. What we have done is gone to another level. We are saying we are going to make things so uncomfortable on this planet, we have to wake up.

Teresa: A lot of my friends in Brussels are going to therapists and trying to understand their problems. Do you think this is a good thing?

Paul: If they are going to therapists, they are starting to look. So, there is movement there, but it is done in a way that is unconscious. If you are going to buy a new car. You usually shop around. You ask your friends what they think of their cars, whether they are reliable or not, how fast they go, etc. You go to the showroom and have a test drive and generally put time and energy into making a decision.

Most people pick a therapist with much less trouble than that. They just hear of one and go there. They don't really look. Then, when they go to the therapist, they somehow give away their authority. They say, "You are the therapist, you are trained, you tell me what I should do." Now, if the therapist is really bad, it is obvious and they change. But if not, they just listen instead of looking at the therapist and saying, "Is your life working? Is what you are telling me working for you?"

If you look, you will find it is not working for most people. They may be doing all right, or managing, but they have got the same troubles in their lives as anyone else and the reason is they are stuck. They are maybe stuck on a slightly higher level, although often the client is more intelligent than the therapist. The therapist has learned certain skills and ways of being with people but most therapists have stopped looking at themselves. If the therapist was still looking, he would not be doing therapy any more. Therapy is just patching up, first aid. It doesn't work. Something totally new is needed. Each person needs to look unceasingly. The client is secondary. The work is secondary. The first thing is discovering themselves. If their lives are about that, it doesn't matter which level of consciousness they have reached. If realizing themselves is their priority, they can share that with the other person and he will move. Therapy is finished. In fact, it is not only finished, it is one of the things that is holding the planet down, because it looks as though it is working and it is not working at all. It's fitting people into a system that does not work. What I am saying at the moment is very difficult because there are very few people who are awake.

Krishnamurti was awake but he wasn't skilled in helping people see themselves. He left it entirely to them. He was one extreme, but he was awake. There are a few people who are awake, not therapists, not people who have skills or experience, but people who have woken up. You need to find somebody like that.

Teresa: Okay! These people also have a great need to feel that they are useful, so they participate in quite a lot of different organizations. They really do want to contribute but I feel there is an energy underneath that.

Paul: What that says to me is that this seed is active but it is still being used in a way to help. You can't help anyone except to the level of consciousness which you have reached yourself. I am not saying that they shouldn't be doing what they are doing. Everything helps, but the main thing is to realize who they are, to find out who they are. All the help on this planet is first aid, it does not work. You just put one plaster on top of the other.

Where do you start? You start right there, you wake up to who you are. You may say, "Well, there are these starving people and the planet is being polluted." But if you really look, you will find you are helping this starvation. You are polluting this planet and you are trying to fix it outside of yourself.

Every one of us is polluting the planet. We are polluting it in the obvious ways with our cars and what we put into the atmosphere, but that is a symptom of our inner pollution. Each of us is polluted. We are polluted by our negative thoughts, by our judgments, by our anger and our lust. We are polluted by everything that is not love.

Scientific experiments are now showing us that each thought has an action. Uri Geller can bend metal without touching it. We are bending metal, we are bending people, we are polluting the planet by our thoughts. We need to get to the place where we don't stop these things because that is just suppression, and what that suppression does is send out condensed waves of negativity which eventually kill us. All the things we suppress become a chemical and kill us in some way. We need to find a way to start to see these things more clearly, acknowledge them, accept them, not suppress them and not put them out. The whole thing starts with each individual, but if you take a look at the time each person invests in himself compared with what he invests in other areas of his life, it is nothing. So, everybody's investing this energy out there, which is sourced in negativity. Most people are more darkness than lightness in their manifestation. Everybody is lightness, everybody is love. But people don't know that and by not knowing that they are perpetuating darkness.

Teresa: I love these people and they are beautiful, but it is true that this darkness, this negativity, is very strong. I can see, when I work with them, that they have really big hearts and they are starving to express that. It is hard in this society to really be yourself.

Paul: We are back to the same thing again. Let me explain something. What I am doing here is, I have a school of people, who although they don't remember it, have done this work in many dimensions on many planets. This school has been around as a team and has gone to planets to help with the transition of consciousness. Now they have come to this planet, and this is one of the most difficult planets in the universe, but they have decided to try the same thing again, so they are being awoken. I have awoken to this and other people have also woken up to who they are and what this planet is about.

We know what is about to happen to this planet. We live in this wisdom. We are also training people who are going to be available when things get really unpleasant here. In fact, we are training people so that enough people wake up, so we don't have to go through the unpleasantness. If people are reading this book, and they really want what I am talking about, they will find me, or somebody like me and they will say, "I am looking at you and I can see what you are saying is your truth. You are living your truth. I want that. How can I get it?" What they will be told is the same thing that every master has ever told anybody who has come up to them, "You have got to want it more than anything else on this planet."

There is a beautiful story about that from the East. It is about a would–be disciple who comes up to a great master and manages to get an interview with him. He says, "I want the truth, and I know that you can show me the truth. Will you take me on as a disciple?" The master says, "Well, this is the time I usually take a swim. Let's go down to the river together and we will talk about it there." They go down to the river and start to swim. Suddenly the master reaches out his hand, grabs the neck of the would be disciple and pushes it under the water. He holds it and holds it and holds it, until the man has given up. Then he pulls him out, looks at him and says, "When you want the truth as much as you just wanted the air, we will start talking."

Until you want the truth that much, you won't find it. It will be a hobby. It will be first aid. It will be something to patch up your life. It won't work. If you really want it, you will find somebody who has already found it, and they will always tell you that you have got to do it yourself. I can give you some ideas, some suggestions and you can come back and talk to me occasionally, but you have got to do it for yourself.

Teresa: Something else that I have been asked often when I go back, when I talk about you and the team, is whether you have a system or method.

Paul: In the past, all teachers or masters who were helping people to realize themselves have had a system. An exception was Krishnamurti, he had no system. He just left you on your own. We are somewhere in the middle, not having a system and not leaving people on their own. We are taking a place in the middle and floating with it. The trouble with a system is that everybody wants to use it as method.

If you want to learn typing, you go to a typing school. If you want to learn computers, you go to a computer college and then you don't do anything yourself. Somebody says, "Press this." And you press that, and you do that. Most people who have learned to drive a car have no idea how a car works.

This is totally different. This is not mechanical at all. You have to wake up to the whole thing yourself. The idea of a system is that it will help you to come out of the fixed place you are in where you are controlled by your neurosis and your conditioning. The problem is that you may come out of your fixed place, but then you become fixed with the system.

The people you are talking about are too intelligent for that, to follow something blindly, just because somebody else said so. But they still want a system, so they can follow it and not have to do it for themselves. You have to do every little bit of it yourself, so no system will work. On the other hand, if I say there is no system, and tell people they have to go away on their own, they don't know where to start. I have travelled the path myself, and I have travelled it in many different ways so that I can understand each person who comes. I can give them some hints, but I can't do anything for them. If I give them a system, they will go away and do the system in the same unconscious way that they are living their lives at the moment. So, what I keep saying is that you have to do it yourself, but here are some hints, here are some things you can try.

What are the guidelines? The main guideline is you have to want to wake up more than anything else. If you don't have that, you are just playing around. The next thing is that you have to be more and more present, here, conscious within the many depths of this moment. So, somebody might say to you, "Do you want to go to so and so?" And you say yes. If you look, you might find there is another level to that yes which might be no. Then there might be a maybe, or I would like to go if... There are levels and levels to this moment. But we are all so mechanical, so automatic, we are living cliches, and we don't look. We need to be here and present and look.

The next thing is that what we are doing in this seminar is something that the world does not do. We tell the truth. You may think that you tell the truth, but if you look, there are levels and levels of truth. If you start to really tell the truth, your whole world will shake. Everything will start to fall apart around you because it is all built up around falseness. You have to see your truth and then have the courage to share it. In the world that is practically impossible for most people because the conditioning is so difficult, so what we have done here is create an environment where that is possible.

We have assembled a group of people who are trained to share their truth, and then they are an inspiration for other people to do the same. When you start to do this, you start to see that your whole life has been built on lies, your lies and other people's lies. Your lies start to be taken apart, and if you keep doing it, you will come right down to the original building block before anyone got to you. Then you will say, "And now I am taking responsibility for myself. I am not automatically accepting anything that anyone is telling me. I am not going to believe them, or disbelieve them. I am going to look at that and see for myself. If I accept it, I accept it for myself."

Then we rebuild ourselves again, in a totally different way from the false conditioning we have had before. We produce an environment of encouragement where people can start to be themselves, where if they are angry they can see that they are angry and acknowledge that, not judge it, not suppress it, not put it out but say, "Now I am angry." And feel what they are feeling. If you do that, you will find out who you are. If somebody insults you, something happens to you and you don't want to feel what happens, and you do something to avoid that. Our whole life is addicted to various forms of things that stop us feeling who we are in each moment. If you are insulted, you are hurt. If you are hurt, you are helpless; and we hate being helpless, so we do something. Somebody insults you, you insult him back. You get angry, you shut off. You ignore him. You get back at him. You feel sorry for yourself, or you go and kick the dog, anything but feel what happened. Now the process of self–discovery is nothing else but saying, "What happened?"

Buddha is said to have had a method where he told his followers to say it three times, "I am unhappy. I am unhappy. I am unhappy." That was just to get you to see what was happening in the moment. "I feel insulted. I feel insulted. I feel insulted." Say it three times so you see what is happening, instead of reacting over the top of it. Just experience yourself in this moment and you will find the next layer. Experience that, and the next layer, and the next layer, and the last layer is God, is freedom, is light, is love. And that is what we are.

In India, they say, "Thou are that." God is said to have said from the burning bush, "I am, I am." Every single being, every single thing, is made up of this substance that has been called God or love. You disconnect from layer after layer of things you have been told, your addictions, your reactions, your automatic responses. If you disconnect from one thing after another, you will be light. You will be being, not even light. You will just be and then you think of angels and choruses. It is nothing like that. It is absolutely ordinary.

It is just, "I am home."

CHAPTER ELEVEN

THE CHALLENGE OF AIDS

An Interview by: Niro Asistent
Hector Hoyles
Steve McCoury
Bartley Cooper

Niro: I am the founder–director of the self–healing AIDS related experiment. Two and a half years ago I was diagnosed with ARC (AIDS Related Complex) and today I dedicate my life to working with people with AIDS. Paul has dedicated his whole life to searching for the truth.

So, Paul, the question that comes right now is that we hear a lot about healing, about healing the planet, about healing the people and here people with AIDS are very concerned about healing. What can you tell us about that?

Paul: Not to interfere. The thing we are talking about, the search for truth, was a search for myself, although I did not realize that at the time. We have to know who we are. We have to look for that intently. When we know who we are, we know what everything is. We interfere, we want to change things. It's just about becoming more aware, more alive and what is supposed to happen, our maximum potential, will happen out of that.

Hector: If one has a very deep feeling that one has learned all the messages that this illness has given us, can one just let it go and get on with one's life?

Paul: Take a look now. You are goal–oriented again, it's what's going to happen at the end. The only thing is what has happened by being here now, choicelessly, and not looking at what is or isn't going to happen outside you.

I suddenly realized who I was. I remembered. I woke up to the fact that there aren't such things as life and death as we see them. We are not born and we don't die. We come into a body, we come into this dimension, but what we call life and death do not actually exist. You find that out by being here now.

If your maximum potential is to stay on this planet longer, you'll stay here longer. You will anyway, the only thing is, do you accept that or do you fight that? If you accept it, you'll have a good time, whatever is happening. If you fight it, you'll be in misery. I understand that you might want to live longer or you want things to be a certain way. The length of time does not matter, it's how present you are within it. If you are present, then you'll finish all the things you need to complete, so at the moment of death you are complete. If you are complete, you are balanced, you are whole, you are one, and then you go to your next level of maximum potential. If you die in confusion, "I did not do this, I did not do that. I upset this person, I am sorry." You will die in that confusion and then you create your next level of wherever you are going. It does not matter about that. That's a long way ahead. Even if it's tomorrow, it's a long way ahead. You have the choice now, to live without your confusion and to live as a balanced being. Now, you can live in what is called bliss. Now.

Steve: If you find yourself in what is called fear, how do you get away from that?

Paul: When we find fear, when we find most things, we want to get out of them. What I am suggesting is, again, be now. You have your fear, that's a fact. You are stuck with it, that's a fact. If you stay with that fear, and stay with that stuckness, you'll give it a chance to alchemize. It will change on its own if it's your maximum potential. If it's better for you to be in fear, you'll be in fear. Maybe you need that fear, maybe you need another level of waking up and this will help you do it. This is what a lot of illness is. It's to help you wake up to the fact that you went to sleep, that you are not realizing what you came to the planet for.

If you are in fear, be in fear. The way out, is in. Keep going in and then you come out. But don't look for the coming out, look for the going in. If there is fear, experience it. Don't make it worse, don't cut it off, just say, "This is what's happening." When it's ready to change, it will change on its own. You don't have to do anything. It changes by acceptance.

I don't experience fear anymore. I now know that there is no life and no death. Everything is just the way it's supposed to be and is doing what it wants to do. I just join in the dance. The last thing for me was not a fear of death, it was a fear of pain, and then that went too. What happened was, I was in incredible pain for months, and during that pain I learned to be there. The body was in pain but I was not in pain any more. A click happened. The body carried on doing what it was doing and I was the watcher. Everything is an opportunity. Everything. You'll mature, you'll deepen and you'll grow if you stay with it.

Bartley: I was very ill for a period of time and it seemed very possible that I might die. During that time, I became aware that I was willing to die, but I was very afraid of continuing to suffer. It bothered me that I was willing to die in that way, because it felt like an escape and not really a complete willingness to die. If I died like that, it would have been like I got out without more suffering or worse pain.

Paul: What happened at that point is that you brought in a little judgment, and it was the judgment that was making you uncomfortable. The game is to see if we can die in balance. If we die in balance, we have already died the way we know it. You die in balance and then you get reborn. Accept it totally and you become accepting, you become choiceless. Then, in that choicelessness, you find you have been reborn to another level of life. Don't try to understand this, just see if you can feel what I am saying. The mind does not go there, so it doesn't understand it.

What you are talking about is very beautiful because you have come to some beautiful levels of awareness in yourself, and you see that to die would have been an escape. This is what you need to do. You need to say, "In this moment I have a choice. I would like to die to escape. I also have a judgment that I would like to die to escape, and I accept the judgment." Don't try and change the symptom. Keep coming back and coming back to the moment. "This is the way I am." The moment you accept the way you are, then you're not that way any more. You are in acceptance, you are in peace. It doesn't matter how you are. As soon as it's accepted, it's in balance. You could call it love. It moves into love and it just becomes a very beautiful vibration. You see if you are aware, if you are there, if you are in that moment, whether you are alive or you are dying, you are balanced. When you are in acceptance, you are in love, and it will be beautiful whether you are alive or whether you are dying, when you slip into the other side.

You cannot go wrong. There is no such thing as wrong. Just be there. "I want to die to escape. I accept that. I want to die to escape." And then suddenly it will change. "This is it. This is it. This is it." With the acceptance you cancel it out. There is no imbalance.

What I am saying is something that cannot be said, so you just have to feel it. Nothing is wrong. Nothing is bad. Nothing is harmful. It's conscious or it's unconscious. With consciousness it's accepting, with unconsciousness it's rejecting.

What I would like you to feel at the moment as a vibration is the following: if you stay present and accepting each moment, whether you are alive or whether you are dying, it's perfect and of course I don't know this for sure, but how I feel right now is it will be perfect. Then, when you accept death in that way, not as an escape but as a choiceless acceptance, you start to live in a totally different way. That is what you and your friends are starting to see, feel and experience. That is why it has been so beautiful being with you. There is a whole new energy with you that most people don't even know exists, a whole new level of love, too.

Steve: I realized I could spend the rest of my life worrying about dying and then go out and get hit by a cab! I have always been a caretaker. I have taken care of my friends and worried about where they are and how they perceive things, especially my family. I have taken care of other people and I find myself often putting them in front of me. I'm trying to get to the realization that in taking care of myself I am taking care of everybody else.

Paul: Until you have woken up to this, you don't know what you are doing when you're taking care of other people. You might be taking care of them when they are going through something they need to go through. When you realize this, you wake up to who you are. When you have accepted yourself totally, you wake up and you see, and then it becomes a caring and not a concern. Most of what we call caring is concern, which means, "I do not want you to suffer because when you suffer I feel bad. I want to put that right over there so that I feel good."

If you come back to yourself and reach your own balance, and then you find what's happening with someone else is not comfortable for you because they are suffering, you don't interfere. You still remain available but you don't interfere. We all interfere because we are trying to fix out there what's uncomfortable in here. Just keep coming back to yourself. When you reach that place in yourself, you just overflow. Even if you don't say anything, even if you don't do anything, you are overflowing with this vibration. Then, when you come, you are appropriate, you come from a place of seeing and not from the mind and from your own pain. When you have accepted yourself, you will find automatically you accept others and then you become appropriate. There is nothing to do. Don't think, "I should not help that person." That's interfering again. If something wants to move there, let it move there but be aware, be there, be present.

"What's happening right now, what am I doing?" Just with that presence you will start to see things differently. You have got something inside you that has a little trip switch. Usually when you reach out, you trip a little switch and then you judge yourself. "Was that right? Was that the best?" Watch your little switch. You cannot do anything wrong, that's just an idea. Wrong and right, good and bad, they are all ideas. Just be, and be as present as much as you know how to be, for the fun of it.

Hector: If one feels complete, but still has a tremendous concern for family and friends, how can we help them with what they may need to go through and at the same time complete that completeness within ourselves?

Paul: When you are complete, you are not concerned about how other people are, although you still care. When you find yourself you become appropriate, you become love. You are not loving, you don't give anybody love. You just love, and if somebody is upset and distressed, you are just there with them. Somewhere they feel that. If a person feels seen, really seen and still feels loved from the other person, a healing takes place, because what's happened is that you have made a circuit for them. Just for a moment, they can accept themselves through you, and then they have to learn to do it for themselves. For a short time they see all the sides of themselves, like their anger and all the things that they don't normally accept, they see them and they still feel they are loved. They feel that they are accepted, and with a real acceptance not a pretended one.

As soon as you lean out you lose it. The person feels the leaning. That means you are leaning out because you do not have it yourself. When all this is going on and you don't come out, they start to slow down. They start to look, they start to pick up the vibration. It may take what you call time, but if you stay in your heart, feeling will happen around you where it is appropriate.

Some people may need to worry about you. That may be the way they wake up. We do not understand on this mind level what is called good and bad and benefit and harm. Just come to that higher Self and you are. And you know exactly what I am talking about. I'm not telling you anything you don't already know. That's what we forget. We keep thinking it's outside. We are told we have to do this and we have to do that and we do not. It's within us now. Everything that is possible in the whole universe is possible there. Now! (points at Hector) You don't have to go anywhere. Get reminded, get woken up occasionally, but you do not have to go anywhere. You just look more and more to yourself, then you find all the truths. They are all inside you.

Bartley: Throughout my experience of this illness, it has come to me many times, that it is not a punishment. That it is a reminder, that it is a waking up of a kind that you cannot ignore. Through this, I have recognized how much energy I have put into ignoring that very message most of my life. I feel now there is a great sense of growth and purpose through this illness and it's very remarkable to me that that can be a possibility.

Paul: Let me just pick up on one thing. You said, "I can't feel it as a punishment." I am suggesting to you that there isn't anyone to punish. There isn't a God in that way. This is it.

Bartley: What struck me was the sense of a possibility of self–punishment.

Paul: That's only out of unconsciousness. If you are conscious, of course you won't punish yourself.

Bartley: Why would you?

Paul: So it's just like a waking up. The other thing that I picked up while you were talking, was that that is a machine. (points to Bartley) It's included in your consciousness, but it's a machine. It's something you have created to move around in this dimension. You did not come here only to take care of the machine. You take care of the machine, of course you do, but you came here for something much more than that. You came here to wake up, to wake up to levels and levels of consciousness. And you can do it quicker when you are in one of these machines. That's why we come. We also come to have fun. It's a great place to have fun.

Niro: Paul, I heard you say you were moved by the people with AIDS that you have been in contact with. Can you speak about the difference between people with AIDS and people with cancer?

Paul: First, I want to talk about being moved. Generally, I am in a different dimension, so I do not feel very much. But every now and again this wonderful feeling comes of being moved, and I have been moved being with you. The difference is somewhere that a cancer patient, and of course I am generalizing here, wants to die. They took on cancer to die. It's a form of unconsciousness that built up an energy it did not want to deal with.

What I am finding now is, the difference with people with AIDS is, and I am not putting this out as a theory but as a possibility, that they gave themselves this out of unconsciousness because they wanted to live. I do not mean that you want to live a long time, but that you want to be more alive. That's what I have found with the people that I have been talking to, a tremendous receptivity, which again touches me. I can feel it coming again now, I feel your heart, I feel your connection. I feel so close to you and I feel so good with you. It evokes this part in myself, it brings the love and I feel your receptivity and that is very beautiful for me.

What I feel with this is that somewhere you want to be more alive, you want to remember more, you want to find your maximum potential and this is one way of doing it. It does not matter whether you gave it to yourself or where it came from. The fact is, this is the possibility and I feel you taking it, and that's wonderful. By doing that, you are going to affect the whole planet. The whole planet is going to benefit from your consciousness because everyone who becomes more conscious sends out a different vibration. It affects people and you know that. The people around you are affected by you, they are touched by you. That's because you have gone to a depth in yourself, and you are helping to heal the planet by your awareness, by your presence, by your acceptance.

Hector: Does this type of awakening happen only when you are desperate?

Paul: It can happen anytime or in any way. We do not listen, so we get a little knock. We still don't listen and we get a bigger knock. Again we don't listen, so we have a car accident and somehow we get well, and we still don't listen! But when you get a terminal illness, you have to listen if you want to live. If you don't want to live, it's a little bit like you were saying before, "Good, I am going to die. I am going to get out of here."

Planet Earth is a difficult dimension. We were all very brave to come here. We could have stayed up there and had a good time playing harps. Anyone, anytime, can wake up. It's easier for some than for others because there are fewer layers on top, there are fewer coverings. But that same spark, that same life, the spark of God, is in everybody. We go to sleep. We get lulled. It can be very thick and heavy. We have to find a way and it is better to volunteer than to wait for something to come along and hit us hard. But you see, this is how you are waking up.

As you know, most people are asleep. You see that now you are waking up. You can start to see their sleepiness. If it is your priority, if you want to live or you want to live longer or you want to get the most out of your time here, you have to be more present and more awake. That way, you are giving to yourself and incidentally you are giving to the planet as well.

Niro: I realized a change in my understanding of healing when I started this experiment. I was very attached to physical healing, but working with so many people who are challenged by AIDS, a new understanding is coming to me. It has to do with the quality of dying. Can you talk about this?

Paul: I will tell you a story about a friend of mine who died of AIDS. We were great friends and we travelled together in many places around the world. Long before we even knew there was such a disease as AIDS, we used to play this game of making sure we did everything we wanted to on this planet, so there was no need to come back unless we wanted to.

So we played this game of completion. Anything we wanted, we got. Anywhere we wanted to go, we went there; anything we wanted to do, we did. Then we discovered that he had AIDS, and he became very ill quite quickly. We went on playing, even though we knew some of the mail order stuff we ordered would not be back before he died. He died so sweetly, so beautifully and so completely. When the energy is balanced and there is peace on this level, we just slide gently into the next.

That is what has been revealed by many people's near-death experiences. If we let go gently, all we do is slide into the next dimension, and then we just carry on. If we fight or we are in distress, that's what we take with us, and it affects that dimension. So the game is to balance as much as possible here and then when the next dimension is ready for us, we just carry on.

Niro: I am really embarrassed to ask this question. It seems a little silly to me. But how do you know that? How come you are so sure?

Paul: On the level we are talking about right now, I do not know it. How can you know about death unless you die? However, there is a way of dying without the body dying. Traditionally, it has been called meditation. Maybe a better description is sitting. Just sitting and watching. And while the watching is happening, the mind's going, the body's doing its thing, the emotions are there, but suddenly you start to see that you are not these things. These things are there, but you are not they. Then you are in another state, a free state, and in that state it is possible to visit, or to become aware of, many dimensions of consciousness. In these dimensions, you can know anything. If you can let go of this dimension, you become available to the others. Then you start to see things that are not normally seen here. So that state of death that I was just talking to you about, I have already been through that, but my body did not die.

I have gone to that place of complete let go, of choicelessness, and that happened. I found I slid into a new dimension, still here, but in a totally different way.

Everything is now relaxed. Everything is easy. Nothing ever gets tight because I realized at that point, that there are no such things as birth and death. The body gets born, the mind gets born, the emotions get born but the being just is. So, if you want to find out for yourself, experiment. Find out your own way, but there is no need to die physically.

Niro: Every time you are talking, I really feel that energy, I feel the connection with you. I tune into it sometimes when I am not with you as well, but I realize it is like a paradox. That energy is so fragile and yet so strong at the same time. My question is, do we need to be exposed to a certain dose until we can really live that way?

Paul: A certain level of vibration has happened to my system. So, when you are in its presence and you are receptive, which means you are not believing it and you are not disbelieving it, you are just available. You start to feel that vibration. But it isn't this system you are feeling, it's that system.(points to Niro) We all have these levels of vibration within us. Mine just starts to resonate yours. Then you start to feel that for yourself and then that's yours. You say that it is strong, but it's very fragile. You don't have it, it has you. If you want to get it, it goes away. You just have to find a way to be there, to be in it. The next thing you say is, you have to be exposed to that. Well, there are no rules, there is no set path.

If you say to yourself one day that the most important thing in your life is, "I want to wake up. I want to find the truth. I want to be free. I want that level of vibration. I want that wisdom." If that becomes your priority, you are halfway home.

From that place, you will then hear everything you need to hear. You will be given all the opportunities you need. As I was sharing with you before, people have said to us as we have gone around, time and time again, "I was just hoping something like this would happen." Or, "I was praying for something like this." When you make this invitation, and it's for a higher level of vibration, you get what you need. It will not always be what you want. You find magically that somebody gives you a book and it's exactly right. Not only that, you can open the book and read it. There's nothing magical about this. There are laws, there are levels of vibration and they are available for anybody who wants it enough.

If that's what you want in order to use it for something, you are not likely to get the help. If you want it because you want to wake up, it just happens. You meet whom you need to meet and you hear what you need to hear. Then, when it happens to you, for most people, you do not really have a choice, it has to be shared. It's like trying to hold back a wild horse. You cannot do it, it needs to go, it needs to share, "Look I have found something. Are you interested, do you want to hear about it?"

Steve: I feel we are in the front lines of a war, because the longer you have been diagnosed with AIDS, the more people you know who are leaving the planet. Something I have been feeling recently is survivor's guilt. Feeling guilty for still being alive and feeling as healthy as I do. I have been fortunate in this whole thing and I have seen many people around me stumbling and falling and trying to grasp on to life.

Paul: Let me try and explain something to you. It's unlikely you will understand it, you might feel it. You might sense it, but you will not understand it. We are creating our reality moment to moment. You have created this because this is what you need. That is what you were saying before, you wanted a video like this, you have created it, you have created this situation. We are creating our reality moment to moment.

We have been programmed by people who do not know anything. They were programed by people who also did not know anything. We have been told what is and what is not, and it is not true.

There is no time and there is no space. There is no such thing as Planet Earth on other levels of realization. We are creating it each moment, every bit of our hearts are creating this dimension because we want it. We came here to learn to have fun, to experience. If you think you are going to die in two years, the likelihood is that you are going to die in two years. You have created it. If people around you with this disease die in two years, this is, in a way, a programming of a death sentence.

You have no idea what is possible. Zen and Buddhism have probably helped more people become realized than any other religions, but even Zen is programming people to time. Two years to learn to sit, two years to learn to breath, twelve years before anything really begins to happen. That's a program. It is not true, it can happen to anybody now. The thing that stops it is our idea of how long it takes and what we have to do. "You have to suffer. You are a poor miserable sinner. You are carrying the sins of your forefathers. You've got to struggle." It's not true, it's just an idea.

There are stories about people who do not die. Jesus is not supposed to have died, it is said he transcended. He can come back anytime he wants to and people say he does. There are supposed to be many masters in the Himalayas who can just come and go because they are not caught anymore in the program in which we are born and we die. Some people say that old age is just programming, that we do not have to die. In fact, I have heard that the medical profession can't quite understand why we age, they do not really know. It's just an idea.

Ideas create our lives in many, many ways. Every thought has a vibration, every vibration has an effect. Think positively, think negatively, you are creating a reality. It's much better to disconnect from your thoughts. Then you start to fly into a different dimension. Do not manifest positively for yourself, because when you do, you create an imbalance. Just be choiceless. "I do not know whether I am supposed to live a long time or not. Does the planet want me, does God want me back, I have no idea."

Just be available each moment, then you will always be at your maximum potential. When you reach that place, there is a great peace that happens inside. There's a balance, a wonderful feeling that happens inside, that says, "Whatever is to be, is to be and I will enjoy that."

Steve: So you are connecting with your true Self when you do that?

Paul: I'd even forget true Self. Forget everything and just say, "I am." Someone said it before out of a burning bush, they said, "I am, I am."

Just be, do not even understand it. When you give up understanding, you'll know. And somehow you'll never know at the same time. It's nothing to do with the mind, you just are. A whole new level of vibration happens around you. Don't think in terms of time and how long and should you heal or shouldn't you heal. Just live consciously and you'll have a good time.

Steve: How do you live consciously when everybody else seems to be so unconscious?

Paul: You have got to want it more than anything else in your life. If you do, you keep catching yourself when you go off. If you want someone's approval, you are going to slip into his or her vibration. If you are still trying for something material, you'll get lost in that.

If you want your consciousness more than anything else, you will keep doing whatever you are doing, but you'll be present. That means you will know exactly where your hands are right now, and how far apart your feet are. You'll be conscious, you'll be here. You'll hear when the air–conditioning comes on. You'll hear the voices in the background. You'll be here. You'll be present to what you hear, what you see, what you feel, what you taste, what you smell. From that moment of awareness, the next thing happens, and then the next and the next. If you want it enough, you have got it, and you know what I am talking about. I am not telling you anything you don't know.

Steve: Yes, I do.

Hector: Is the resistance that we experience whenever we think of dying or of death out of the programming that we were discussing earlier?

Paul: If you take a look, you'll see that for yourself. You are programmed to think that death is not a good thing, that there are all sorts of terrible things, that you can go to hell or you can go to oblivion and that it's painful and that it is uncomfortable. You pick up the vibrations of death from the mourners, who are not mourning for the one who died but for how unhappy they are that the person isn't there any more. It's about themselves.

Disconnect from everything you have been told, including what I am telling you now. Disconnect from everything and say, "I am going to find out for myself. I am going to look for myself. I am not going to go against you because that is a way of getting caught up with it. I am not going to disbelieve you because that is the opposite of believing, I am going to look for myself, I am going to float my doubt. I don't know whether anything is true unless I see for myself." Look for yourself. The conditioning is there, the programming is there. Don't fight it, just acknowledge it. "Yes, that is there."

Let everything become calm and still and then look and you will know. There is no such thing as time. Who you are going to be, you already are. You have chosen to exist as a vibration in this dimension, but the other dimensions are also available to you.

The original meaning of prayer was just an opening, but now we get down on our knees and beg to something higher. There is nothing to beg to, there isn't anything higher. You have different levels of vibration that are available to you now. You can call it your inner voice or your higher Self. Some people call it ascended masters. It does not matter what you call it, that information is available to you. You do not have to beg. You can just say, "I feel ready for that now. If that's appropriate I would like to know." And you will know.

Hector: When you talk about spiritual guides, who are you talking about?

Paul: Okay, everything I have told you today is not true. Everything I told you in the last interview is not true. What is true cannot be said. What I attempt to do is bring this vibration in, and see if I can translate it in a way that you can vibrate with it, so that you remember for yourself. I do not want to tell you anything. You have been told enough. Just vibrate with that energy. That's why I say to you so often that you already know that. We know that, but we are so busy with what we have been told, we do not listen to ourselves.

One of the levels or one of the descriptions is guides. You have a guide and the guides have guides. That is true and in another way it is not true at all. It is a way of trying to talk to somebody about something. What I suggest is, do not go to the guides because, in a way, when you do, you are saying that your guide is more than you. The guides are learning as much from you as you are possibly learning from them.

What I am saying is, if you get an image of a guide you are stuck with that. If you get an image of Christ you are stuck with that. So, you often find that when people have a religious experience that they have it according to their religion. A Buddhist sees Buddha and a Christian sees Christ, but that is a contamination of a pure energy. Christ is not the ultimate, Buddha is not the ultimate, they are just forms which have become a little bit more solid, to take a look at.

Don't get stuck there. Don't get stuck anywhere. Just say, "I am available for the ultimate." Why settle for a Ford when there is a Ferrari available? You are not being arrogant, you are just saying, "Thank you very much for all the levels available. I am here." Do not identify with them. As soon as you identify with them you fix them. Don't do that because there may be another level and then another level. If you open to that, if you become truly choiceless, one day you will realize yourself.

Many people have come to the planet this time to become realized, to help the planet in a change of consciousness. They have come to wake up. And then the game is how they are going to do that, because people are not only sleeping, they are dreaming they are awake. They do not want to be woken. Many of us have come to the planet this time just to help people wake up, so the sooner you wake up, the sooner you can start playing that game. Also, when you wake up, all the experiences you have been through create a vibration in you. So, when you work with people who have a terminal illness you are going to be more effective than somebody who has not been through that, because you have healed that part in yourself. Here I do not mean the body, I mean the vibration in you that you have healed.

Somebody who has never been addicted to drugs does not really have a connection with somebody who has, he does not really understand him. If you have been through that and come out of it, you have that connection, you have that understanding. Every experience we go through becomes a maturity for ourselves and an availability for other people.

Bartley: One of the things that has been very present for me in this experience is the effect of the other people around me in my life, what they have given me, and also what I have been able to give them.

We spoke before about the intensity of the moment and being present. I find now, having really thought that I might die and also the people around me believing that was very likely, that my relationships with these people have altered considerably. The quality is much finer and there is much less negativity involved. I feel that it is a blessing and a cleansing of so many things in relating to people, and I wonder if you might say something about this?

Paul: The first thing I have to say to you is not actually to do with that. Whenever I tune in to you, I feel touched. I love you and I feel love there. You have gone to this place of almost dying and come back, and you have come back with a dimension of love. It has woken up in you. There is something very beautiful around you, and that is what is affecting people. It then reflects off them and comes back to you. It goes backwards and forwards. Something very beautiful has happened to you.

Bartley: I feel that very strongly.

Paul: That affects people and it is helping them to see. I have been going around seeing many people, many accomplished people, many famous people. Most of them are afraid to live in the place where you live all the time, with a soft gentleness, with this openness, with this availability. When you walk in the door, you bring another level of vibration. You affect everything around you because you have allowed a let go in yourself. You have been to the edge of death, you have seen something and you have brought something back with you.

There is nothing to do and there is nothing to say. Just allow that to be with you deeper and deeper, and don't understand it. When you feel love for somebody or something or anything, just be like a flower, just let the perfume...

CHAPTER TWELVE

THE HEALER WITHIN

An Interview by Don Pachuta M.D.

Don: We talk about being the victims of disease or illness, and catching some virus or bacteria from something or someone. Perhaps you might say a word about the nature of healing. Also how do people get sick, how do they get cancer or AIDS or disease in general?

Paul: Let me give you a different perspective. When you wake up to who you are, you see. When you see, you see that the way you have been seeing in the past is distorted. We are born and we do everything we can to survive, to be as comfortable and as happy as possible, and to make this dimension work.

When you see, you know that this dimension isn't about that, it isn't supposed to work. If it worked, you would go to sleep and you wouldn't look. You put yourself here as a challenge to find out who you are, where you have come from, and where you are going. That is what you came for.

In the process of putting yourself here, you gave yourself a program, and that program included what you call unpleasant situations. In these situations you are more awake, more aware, and you are more likely to look. So, a lot of the things that happened to us, we chose so that we could grow and expand and become fuller through the experiences. Another way of looking at illness is that when we are born, we are born to expand, born to move, born to grow. What happens is we stop, and then that energy keeps moving inside. If we don't grow, the energy goes on inside and some people say that's what cancer is, it's growth. You didn't do it, so the body is doing it.

That energy that you don't allow to flow backs up inside you. If you get angry or resentful, or hurt, and you don't find a way of moving that emotion, it builds up inside and then the system can't work the way it was designed to. This is a self–healing system, but we need to allow it to do that. That includes doing the healthful things that are needed.

Don: What are some of those healthful things?

Paul: I could give you hundreds of things, but then you are going to have to have a book and look them up. You don't need a book, because if you are here, you are now, you are present and honest, you will know exactly what is healthful and what is damaging. You know that. Nobody is stupid. We become stupid and we act stupid, but everyone is that divine supreme intelligence. We are that. But in order to be in touch with that intelligence, we have to be here, we have to be present.

The trouble is, our computer, our system, has been programmed with many programs that are not helpful. They have been put there by people who are sick. We have to disconnect from these programs and start to listen to ourselves. When you reach out for that drug, that drink, that chocolate, if you listen, you will know whether it is appropriate for you or not. If you listen you always know. If you start lifting something that is too heavy, you know that. If you are driving too fast, you know that. If you are having an argument that is creating a destructive energy, you know that. Normally, we are too fast, we are too into doing and so we just go crashing through these barriers and then we have to take the consequences. You talk about the victim and that is the way we live. We live in complaint and that's just unintelligent. If you stop and you look, you will see that you have created everything. If you hadn't said that final word, she wouldn't have thrown the saucepan.

Don: That's for sure! It is amazing though, that we don't want to accept or acknowledge that. We don't want to take responsibility when we get sick, even when we have a cold, we still say we caught it.

There is an enormous amount of negativity and fear surrounding illnesses like cancer and AIDS, and intrinsic to the process of healing is the dealing with the fear. We are doing something with the AIDS epidemic that we have not done before. Influenza, tuberculosis and polio were highly contagious and doctors were fearless in the past when dealing with these diseases. AIDS is not at all contagious, except by sex, blood or drug abuse, yet doctors are so afraid that they are going to get AIDS.

Paul: Let's deal with the first thing. It's not just fear, it is terror and it is terror of dying. The reason is that we have forgotten who we are. This body is an earth suit. In order to be on this planet, in this dimension, we have had to adopt something material. More and more people are starting to experience that they are not their bodies. They either leave their bodies, or have a near–death experience and find that they are out of the body. Many people come out of their bodies when they are on the operating table having surgery or in dreams and in other situations. They are starting to see that they are not the body, that the body is a vehicle. If you are identified with the body and you get caught up in the fear, you can disconnect from that, you can say, "Yes, the body is upset, the body is ill, but I'm not ill." Then there is not so much fear.

Don: What about the cultural fear that seems to be present in the AIDS epidemic?

Paul: There are several layers to do with that. One is that this planet is being given a hard time in many ways and that is because it wants to change. It wants to upgrade itself in consciousness, and in order to do that, it's making things a bit worse first. It's a bit like giving something a homeopathic dose. It's got to have a little bit more, because if it stays the same it will stay asleep. Give it a bit more, make it a little worse and people will start to wake up more. A lot of what is happening, including AIDS, is to make things a little worse so that people start to look.

Don: I am a physician, I practice medicine and have a specialty in infectious diseases, so I see a lot of people with AIDS as a result of that. Also, I work with guided imagery and such techniques so I see a fair number of people with cancer. All of those kinds of major diseases going around today seem to be violations of our own immune system. Somehow we have lost the ability to simply allow our immune system to work. Here is a virus that can't even live outside the body and yet it is doing this devastating thing called AIDS.

Paul: We could say we have lost the will to live. We could say it is a form of suicide for the planet and in one way that is true. The planet wants to die as it is, it wants to be something else. It doesn't want to go on being uprooted and raped, and it doesn't want to go on living in violence.

The planet is a living thing. We are part of it. Just like this finger is part of my body. We are part of this planet and it's tired of this. It wants to upgrade, so part of it is saying we have to wake up.

You were mentioning on a previous interview I did that I said that for people who get AIDS, there is a program that says they have six months to two years to live, and that isn't necessarily true. I don't care about that. It doesn't matter whether a person dies or not. It matters whether they live or not, and often, challenging situations will bring them alive. Some of the most alive people I have met are people with AIDS. Just last night we were with a group of people who had AIDS and I haven't had questions like that anywhere before. When they ask a question, they are there. It's life and death for them, and sure there is death, but there is also life. It doesn't matter whether you live for six months or two years or one hundred years. It's the quality of living that matters and most people aren't living, they are dying. What you said about the immune system is absolutely right. We are a self healing system and we have some control over it.

It is no good saving a person if he hasn't got a will to live. He will just find another way to die. The main thing is not curing the illness, it's waking up the being. Once the being is awake it will say, "Do I want to live longer?" If it does, it will live longer. Nothing can stop it. We create our own reality moment to moment. If you want to live you will live.

Don: How do we wake up the being? I have heard you say before that the immune system is loving, and that love stimulates the immune system. How do we wake ourselves up?

Paul: We haven't had any encouragement up to now. We have been told we are poor miserable sinners, everything we do is wrong, we are carrying the sins of our forefathers, everything is going upstream. And this isn't true. Many of the things we are told are not true, like you pointed out to me before when I said people with AIDS have only two years to live. Some people have cured themselves of AIDS, so it isn't true. Nothing is actually true.

We create truth. What we need to do is live more alive, be more alive, when we meet, meet. If you really meet somebody love happens, and a healing takes place. If we as individuals start to live more consciously, we start to live more moment to moment, we then affect each other as we move around. People then have their programs shaken. For example, nobody had cured himself of AIDS so it was fatal. Now a few people have cured themselves so it isn't necessarily fatal any more. There are many other things we are fixed with. If we start bringing our consciousness there and we see, it changes.

Don: How do we translate that into a sort of day–to–day program, not just for people with AIDS or cancer, but for people who don't want to get AIDS or cancer, or anything else like that?

Paul: This is the way I did it. Over and over again, many times in the day I said, "Do I want to be here? Do I want to be now? Do I want to be doing what I am doing?" If I wasn't, I got out. It didn't matter how much money I lost or how many people got upset, I kept taking care of this. (points at himself) Many people are in relationships, are living in houses, districts, countries that are destructive to them. It is no good talking to the masses of people who aren't yet awake enough to see this. However, there are millions of very intelligent people who could change their lives today, and say, "I am not going to be in this situation anymore, it's destroying me. I'm out, whatever it costs."

"Do I want to be in this interview right now?" If I didn't, it wouldn't matter how many cameras were around or how much we paid for the studio, I am out. If I don't want to be here, I will not be here, because then I am destroying something in myself and I am not living my own truth. If you live your truth moment to moment, you won't be ill, you won't need to be ill.

Don: Yet we really, really resist that. We were saying just a minute ago that love is the natural condition and we need to love ourselves. Yet I see people day–to–day, myself included, resisting the notion of loving themselves. It seems so hard, so many barriers are in the way.

Paul: Loving yourself is a big jump. The first thing is to learn to accept yourself. Love follows. To accept. "I was just unconscious then. I caused some pain in that person. I did that, now I am here. I have learned from that, I am here." But we judge ourselves, we go and sit with it. "I shouldn't have done that, and anyway they created it." We go through all this stuff instead of just finishing with the past.

Finishing and starting again. That's one of the things that Zen said, "Every second is the first second of your life." And it is, unless you go to the mind which is connected to acres of past. The past just kills you. The present brings you alive. Keep being here and saying, "I am here no matter what I have done. I am here. I am here. I've just upset that person, I will buy her some flowers or send her some chocolates. I'll finish that, but now I am here. I start my life now."

Don: Intrinsic to that, of course then, is to have cancer or AIDS or whatever else you have, and be okay with it.

Paul: To become choiceless, because you can't do anything anyway. Christ is quoted as saying, "Thy will be done." It will anyway. It doesn't matter whether you say yes or no. It'll happen. It's the only choice we have. We say yes to it or we say no to it. If we say yes to it, we are in the flow and then we start to expand. If we expand, we heal, if we say no, we contract. When we contract we stop everything. The nerves contract, the blood vessels contract, everything contracts and you can't heal yourself. In expansion, if it's appropriate you will heal yourself, healing will happen on its own. Now I am not saying don't go to a doctor or take the drugs he recommends, and I am not saying don't take the precautions, but all these things will work faster and be more effective if you are in expansion. If you contract with fear, you will hold up the system. If you expand, "This is what is happening with me, I have contracted cancer. Now, what does that mean to me? Do I want to live or do I want to die? Did I bring this on unconsciously? Do I want to go on doing that? What do I need to do? I need to consult a physician, I need to follow the advice. I need to take a look at what I am breathing, at what I am eating, what I am thinking. I need to take a look at everything and ask myself how I can produce a healing environment with what I have got." If you waste your time saying, "I shouldn't have done this, I don't want this," you will just contract and healing becomes very difficult.

Don: In what you have just said, there is a major point to be made. Healing is also the healing of the self, the spirit, not necessarily the healing of the disease. There is a parable about that in the Bible involving ten lepers. All ten were cured and the one man who came back to say thank you was the man to whom Christ said, "You are healed." We don't often look at it that way, do we?

Paul: That's beautiful. Physicians very often heal people's bodies, but they sometimes go and create something else, because it hasn't gone through the levels, it hasn't healed the source. The source is deeper than the body and it is that source that produces health or produces disease. Then we do have to look at that, we have to change our priorities.

Don: It certainly seems that that might be one of the most difficult barriers. Often I see people with cancer or with AIDS or some disease like that, and I ask them if they would like to devote one hour a day to their inner healing by doing some meditation, or listening to some relaxation tapes and it's not an automatic yes among a lot of people.

Paul: As I said, there isn't the support for that yet. As each individual starts to live that, it just moves to another person and then another person, and it starts moving that way.

Don: You mentioned choicelessness before and perhaps that notion may be difficult for some people to understand. Can you expand on that a little, and give a couple of examples?

Paul: Yes it is difficult. Let me go back to one thing first that includes choicelessness. If I am the doctor and you are the patient, and then you come along with cancer, my heart will be with you. I would like to see you well, but I am choiceless about that. Maybe you need not to be well, maybe you need this situation and I can't see that, so I will not be concerned about you. I will care and I will do everything that is possible, but if you decide not to do that hour a day, I will still do everything I can. The choicelessness in me becomes a love for you. It's not a condition that if you are not going to do this hour, then I am not going to treat you. I am not going to be offhand with you, because nobody is making a mistake or doing anything wrong on purpose. It's just unconsciousness, it's just your conditioning. It's the love that heals, so if you don't want to do an hour, then let's see if we can settle for a half–hour. If you don't want to do a half–hour, let's take a look at you doing fifteen minutes.

Don: That's an incredible notion, not just for physicians, but for everyone else too, letting people make whatever choice they are making, and not enforcing our preference. Most of us who are physicians won't say, "Well, I am not going to see you if you are not going to do that hour." But we do have something on a vibrational level that says they are not okay.

Paul: What I would do in that situation is be very honest and tell the patient that this is how I see it, and explain that if he doesn't do that, he will make it more difficult for himself and more difficult for me. "This is what I see you need, if you don't want to do that, that's fine." Guilt is poison, to make anybody feel guilty is poison. It's just going with what is. Love is the healer and if you are loving yourself, it emanates from you.

Don: Maybe just a word about that notion, love is the healer, and the connection with the divine within. We ignore that we have this stubbornness as you said earlier. We are convinced that we are all sinners and of course if we just had a glimmer of the divine within, we might not be that way.

Paul: Ask for it. The old–fashioned way was to pray and to me that was ugly. Prayer is ugly because it is begging to somebody. There is no need to beg, there is nothing greater than you. There is a God, but he is not any greater than you are, because you are also God. Ask, just say, "I would like a glimpse of that. My doctor has just told me I need to meditate and somehow I can't meditate. Is there anybody or anything that can be a help for that?" Try that, especially just as you are going to sleep. Sleep is a great healing power at the moment. If you are ill and you are just going to sleep, you can say, "I am open for any suggestions, I am open for any help." Often, when you wake up in the morning, you will find you have a message which will help, so if you need help you can ask.

Don: What would you say if you were President of the United States or Emperor of the World or something similar? What would you say to everybody in terms of how he should react to other people who are on the planet, especially on AIDS? It seems that AIDS is testing the very mettle of this country at the moment.

Paul: First of all, I wouldn't talk to everybody. I would talk to the very intelligent people, the crystalized people, the people in power, the people with money, the people in control. It's these people who are going to affect the world and if they start looking, and they start being loving it will start to move very fast. If the emperor is loving, he will have loving people around him.

Don: "Let there be peace on Earth, and let it begin with me," as the song says. If I summarize what you are saying it seems to be about becoming awake, becoming more aware and then accepting and loving yourself.

Paul: And taking it as a hypothesis that there is something else to wake up to, you are more than you know.

Don: So we are more than just our little shells.

Paul: Much, much more.

CHAPTER THIRTEEN

COMMENTARIES ON JESUS

An interview by Monny Curzon

Monny: I sometimes find it irksome in spiritual circles how much emphasis is placed on sayings of the Eastern masters such as Buddha, Lao Tsu, and the Zen masters, and comparatively little on Jesus. It seemed to imply that Eastern mysticism was Hipso facto better than Western. While Jesus of Nazareth could hardly be called a Westerner, certainly not a member of the European community, he nevertheless has been our man for the best part of two thousand years. He died, was misinterpreted, was loved, and adored, and in the process covered our countries with incontestably the finest and most beautiful mystical buildings in the world. Therefore, it's really encouraging how often you cite the sayings of Jesus. Could you talk about some of his better known sayings?

Paul: Let me just say one thing first. You said that so often the quotations are from the East. One of the reasons for this is that there are many more realized people in the

East and a tradition has built up there. If we take Buddha, he had his realization, and then somebody else caught that from him, who in turn helped someone else. So there was a line for five hundred years of realized people, then there was a break and then it came back again. These masters were effective in helping many others to become realized and that is one of the reasons why the New Age is looking there.

Monny: How do you interpret, "Seek and ye shall find, knock and it shall be opened unto you?"

Paul: Generally, I think Jesus was talking a language that the people around him had a possibility of understanding. What I find with myself is, if somebody asks me a question, I open to the answer and then it comes very clearly and obviously. When I try to connect it with the person who's listening, sometimes I feel that this person will misinterpret what I say. Even the word "love," a word that we all use so many times, is understood by different people in different ways on many, many different levels. I often think that when Jesus was saying something, he was the same as all realized people, and making a compromise between what is the truth and what the person could start to glimpse.

He says, "To knock." In a way that's an aggression. There's no need to knock. I know exactly what he means. He is saying, to make the invitation, make the effort, be available and it's already there. When he says, "It shall be opened." That isn't actually true because it's never been closed. It's a way of trying to express something so people can understand. Nothing has ever been closed, nothing has ever not been the ultimate.

Bankai was from the East and he was a Zen master. His teaching was called, "the unborn." What I understand from what he said is that the Kingdom of God, the ultimate, was never born and it will never die, it is. Our bodies are born, our bodies die but this energy is, and it is in each person. There's no need to knock and there's no need to seek. It's an opening, an availability, it's an invitation. It's just saying, "I'm ready." When you say you're ready, it has to be unconditional. If you say, "I'm ready, providing I can stay in this job, with my partner or with my children or with my money," that condition is in the way. Whether or not you need to leave your family or possessions, you have the condition.

I'm just remembering another quotation from Jesus, "Unless you leave your father, your mother, your sisters, your brothers and your wives and your children, you will not enter into the kingdom." He wasn't saying you have to leave them. He was saying you have to become detached, you have to stop leaning on them and using them to fill in a place that's empty within yourself. So when he says, "To knock, or to seek," I don't interpret that as if we have to bang on someone's door or go off looking. It's here, it's now, the Kingdom of God is within. We need to make ourselves available.

Monny: And, "Suffer little children, forbid them not. Unless you become like one of these, you are not wise."

Paul: Such a beautiful way of putting it. We have all become crafty, cunning, clever and manipulative in order to survive. We have gone a certain way with our lives, which was intended, so that we could investigate every dimension in which we live. We went into the darkness to experience that and now we've got stuck there. It's time to come back. The children are the innocent ones but it's not that most children are innocent because they are not. In order to survive, they had to become cunning.

A child needs total, unconditional attention and the parent doesn't know how to do that because he doesn't have the time, he doesn't have the patience, he was never taught that himself. The child has to survive, and in order to do that she has to get the parent's attention, because she needs love as well as food to survive. She needs caring because she isn't yet able to look after herself, so she becomes cunning. Often, when she is natural and does what she wants to do, she gets punished because she is too noisy, messy, or destructive. So she becomes cunning and starts to think, "What am I allowed to do, and what am I allowed not to do?" Then she stops being as Jesus means a child.

A child is very innocent. It does not think, it is. Like that beautiful cartoon you showed me the other day of the man and the dog. The bubble for the man was, "Thinking." For the dog, which could also easily have been a small child, it was, "Ising." It doesn't think.

"Suffer the little children that come unto me." The innocent ones, not the stupid ones, not the dull ones, not the boring ones, because a child is not boring and it is not stupid. Before it has been corrupted it is very intelligent. It has the spark of life and adventure in it, but it is innocent. It doesn't know. Every time it looks, it does so without knowing. When it looks at a flower it doesn't say, "This is a flower." It just looks and becomes one with the flower. There is no barrier between the child and the other, there is no I and there is no thou. They are just "ising." When Jesus says, "Suffer the little children, to come unto me."

It is the ones who are present, the ones who are here, the ones who don't have the barrier of knowledge.

Monny: And those are the ones who will enter the Kingdom of Heaven?

Paul: They are already in the Kingdom of Heaven. When a being is innocent, it is in the Kingdom. The cat is there, it is in bliss, but it does not know that. What we decided to do by coming to this planet was to forget and work, to remember our way back home. The reason for this was so that when we entered this place again, we would be aware of this bliss and then have a whole new dimension of appreciation. We had experienced the opposite, not just seen it from a distance or been told about it, but experienced the misery. We work our way back home, but the child is already home. It's born in that but doesn't realize it. A child doesn't know that, so it has to lose it in order to regain it and appreciate it. The fish doesn't know it is in the water until it is thrown out. When it is out, it knows what the water is, and when it comes back in again, it appreciates the water.

Monny: You mentioned the difficulty that family life is going to present for a seeker. In the words of Jesus, he has to leave his father and mother. What about the commandment, "Honor thy Father and thy Mother?"

Paul: When you have reached a deep acceptance of yourself, you stop judging yourself and you see yourself for what you are in each moment. When that happens, you start to see other people in that way and you no longer judge them. You have looked and looked and looked and the judgment melts away. As it melts away with yourself it melts away with other people. If you continue with the process, the acceptance moves into something else, which is love. You become appreciating, you become loving. At the moment that happens deeply within you, it happens to another. Then usually there is a little process where the sensitivity in the mind moves around and when it sees the parent, it has gratefulness that these people did what they did. They put themselves through what they did to bring this being into this dimension, so that it could do the work that it needed to do, which could be either for itself or for others. There is a realization, an opening, a seeing and an appreciating. If we use the word honor, which means put them up and put yourself down, then I find that degrading. Nobody is up and nobody is down. Nobody. Not the violent person who is on the street, not the so–called innocent person who is attacked, there are no differences between any of us. The only difference is whether we are awake or asleep to who we are. The way I interpret honor is to see the other, so when you see a flower you honor it, when you see a bird you honor it. It has nothing to do with a status or an equality.

Monny: What you say of judgment recalls the work we do here in the meditations, where we are trying to look at the judgment we place on other people and other situations. So what of Jesus saying, "Judge not and ye be not judged?"

Paul: It is a wonderful saying and it has so many depths to it. In order to understand these depths, you have somehow got to empty the mind a little and become more neutral. "Judge thee not, less ye be judged." If you are not judging, you will never be judged even if somebody is judging you. If they are judging you and you are not judging that judgment, you don't see it as judgment. This person is "ising." He is doing the best he knows how to do with his level of awakeness, with his level of consciousness.

When you have reached this place of acceptance in yourself, you reach this place of acceptance with someone else. When you stop judging here, you stop judging there and then you never see judgment because judgment does not exist for you. This person has an action, he is doing something, but you won't label it with the word judgment because it doesn't exist for you anymore. That person is just doing what he is doing.

Monny: I remember when I was seven years old, we had to draw the "Sermon on the Mount, and there was one Beatitude that went through me like an arrow. That was, "Blessed are the pure in heart for they shall see God." Would you like to comment on that?

Paul: We are all pure in heart, but we have covered up the heart with all these levels of experience. Once you have had an experience it is finished, but we do it again and again and become addicted to it. These become layers on the heart. "The pure in heart." The way we are working with it here is to be truthful, so if you have a thought or a judgment, you share them. See if you can share them with as little judgment as possible for the other and for yourself. Just reveal yourself. As you do this, you start to accept yourself and then you stop avoiding so much. You stop avoiding negative thoughts. You allow them, but you don't energize them and you don't suppress them. This allowing neutralizes and they die away.

As this process happens, you become more silent, more still and sensitive. In this sensitivity, you start to become aware of all those little thoughts that are a contamination to your being, that bring impurities to the heart.

Just this very awareness starts what Jesus would call purifying the heart. In essence, the heart is already pure and what you are doing is taking the layers away. Purity is always within everyone, it is always there.

You come down through the layers to the heart and the moment you reach this purity you are God, you are one with God because God is the purity. As you reach that purity in yourself, you will realize you are not separate.

Jesus is a contamination of God, he is a slightly lower vibration than God. He did that so he could make a communication between this level and that level. In order to make that connection, he lowered his vibrations so far down that he became what we call human. He came into a body. After he died, he started to raise his vibrations up again so they became higher, and he ascended. He allowed his vibrations to increase, to become finer and finer, and as they reached a certain level, the solid disappeared. It wasn't, "Dust to dust." It was molecules to molecules. They just went back home into their natural state, and his being went into a finer state.

Jesus is still around this dimension. He comes through certain people. What we are doing here is training people to be available for that energy. He is around because this planet hasn't made its transition yet. When it has, he will allow his vibrations to go even finer and he will be back in the One, which is God.

Monny: "I am the way, the truth and the light. No man comes unto the Father except through me."

Paul: What he is talking about is a state of being. The way he put it was a way that the people around him could understand. I think he dropped his vibrations a little bit too low there. It was fine for the people around at that time, but it wasn't very good for the people who followed later. That is when he became a cult, when people started to follow somebody. Jesus is not a somebody, Christ is a state of being and this state of being is within all of us. What he is saying is, "Unless you follow me, unless you come to this state of vibration which is me, and is also in everybody, unless you realize that state in yourself, you won't enter the Kingdom."

He is saying you can't do it the way you are trying to. You can't do it through your materialism or just going to the synagogue on Friday or Sunday. It has to be something that is within you every moment, that is looking for that purification.

So, what I understand him saying is, the only way to come back home is to go through these levels, and he is a representative of that state.

Monny: In doing your work and spreading what you have to say and your state of being to as many people as possible, it brings to mind his possible last pronouncement, "When two or three are gathered together in my name, I will be with them."

Paul: (...silence...) This silence now is because I feel him here. Again, it is not particularly Jesus, it is that state of energy. He does come, his uniqueness comes. It is a slightly softer level of vibration that makes Jesus different from Buddha, Sanat Kumara or Gurdjieff or any of the other realized people. Each one has his uniqueness. When you hear me talk as I was talking yesterday, that is the energy of Sanat Kumara. (The Aging and Dying interview) When you feel me talking like this, this is the energy of Jesus. It's very gentle, very loving, very caring.

"When two or three are gathered together in my name." By bringing a few people together, another level of energy is created that is much more powerful. On our own, we keep getting lost in the mind, and that isn't enough to manifest that energy within us and around us.

When we come together, we are not particularly calling Jesus, or Buddha or anyone else. What we are doing is saying we are available for a higher level of vibration, and the level that comes is the one that is appropriate for us. If we need the energy of Jesus at that time, Jesus comes. If we need the energy of Buddha, Buddha comes. Krishnamurti has joined the team now as well, and he is around to be with us. This coming together is a reminding, a binding of this energy that becomes more powerful.

It's stronger in a small group, but it is not enough that we keep relying on the group. We need to become so aware, so available, and so pure, that some of this energy is with us always. Then, when we walk into a shop, we have the compassion of this level of vibration with us. When we talk to a shopkeeper or a ticket collector or anybody, we are that level of vibration. That is what is healing, whether the person remembers or not. All that has happened with this person is that he has forgotten who he is. You come with your love and compassion and your gentleness and caring and it affects this being. It helps the person to wake up to who he is.

Jesus had another saying which is one of the most powerful for me, "Seek you first the Kingdom of God and all else is added on to you." Again, this is often misinterpreted. He is not saying that when you have attained the Kingdom of God, all else is added on to you. What he is saying is, "Start seeking and you are already there. Make yourself available, and it has already happened." He didn't say, "When you have attained, you have everything." If you seek, everything will happen for you. You will be blessed, you will be showered, you are on the way home and you have to be taken care of. Jesus in his other state will take care of you, he will make sure everything is supportive and helpful, because you are on the way home.

If anything else is more important to you than seeking the Kingdom of God, then you are not on the way home. It does not matter how many times you go to Church, or how many times you meditate.

As soon as it is your priority, then you really start to enjoy this dimension.

Monny: We have sometimes talked of the question of evil and clearly the Church makes much play of the exclusiveness of some of Jesus's remarks. "Only through me, the only begotten son." It places a great emphasis on the duality between that path, the Church's path, and the devil's path. It brings us back to Jesus saying, "Resist not evil." How do you interpret that?

Paul: Any resistance becomes a suppression and it stays in your system. Two things happen. One is, it kills you, and that's what diseases like cancer, arthritis and rheumatism are, they are energies that need to be expressed. Energy is material, thought is material. Everything is solid. It is more solid or less solid. A repressed thought, let alone a repressed action, goes inside and produces an effect and a chemical that kills you. The very resistance of it just condenses it inside.

Another level is this: if you resist it, you are tucking it away somewhere, you are not dealing with it. What he is saying is, allow. "Judge ye not." Be choiceless, allow it to come, this is you at the moment. You like to think that that shouldn't be you, but it is. See it. Don't resist the evil, take a look at it. If you look at it and accept it and you allow it to be, you will find you are less judgmental of it. If you stay with it, it will just disappear. Go right into the center of it. Stay there. Have the courage to see all the darkness in yourself and go there and go there, and then there is light. If you continue through light, you will find there is no light and there is no darkness. It is part of the duality. There is an "isness" that can't be understood. Evil is not inside. Evil does not exist anywhere in the universe, except within our minds. Think evil and you will produce evil, be with the light and you will be in the light. What we call evil is within our minds, every time someone talks about evil as something outside, they are creating evil within themselves. We are the creators. God produced in the image of himself. If we think of evil, we will create evil. If we be with love, we will allow love to happen.

Monny: You and I, almost all of us here, were brought up in the Christian tradition. I wouldn't expect you to see yourself as a Christian or as a member of anything but I am wondering how you feel about Jesus as Christ?

Paul: I love Jesus. I love his compassion, his gentleness, his love, his caring and his incredible patience. He took on himself a very difficult job that he didn't have to take. He was already clear of that energy. He had no karma and he volunteered to come into this dimension. He volunteered to die, to try and wake us up to show us something, and it worked for a few, but mostly what happened was the dark side of each person took over and turned his message into Churchianity.

The Church has not to do with Christ anymore. There might be a few people who call themselves Christians who are in touch with Jesus, but the Church as such is not in touch with him. It's become another level of politics. Like most of the so–called "great religions," it started from somebody pure and then became contaminated. We love to follow, so someone else is taking care of things. We pay him a salary and he looks after it for us. We have to take that back now. We have to look at everything we have been told. We must read the Bible with our hearts and not with our minds. The Bible is not true. It has been contaminated, parts have been taken out, it has been interpreted and misinterpreted. The Kingdom of God is within. Now. It is there in each of us and there is no within and there is no without, there is just ...is.

When you see, you will realize for yourself, you will be a Christ and more. When you read the Bible, you must allow something to leap across to remind you what you already know. Don't accept what I am saying. Don't accept anything from anybody automatically. Come with your heart, not with your mind. Your mind has been conditioned, it has been told what is right and wrong and good and bad and benefit and harm. Forget it, it is not to do with the mind. Your heart knows. Your heart is pure because it cannot be impure. It has never been impure, it just needs reminding. It just means going through those levels and being in touch with the heart and taking responsibility for yourself. Don't follow anybody or anything. Look for yourself, "Seek and you shall find."

Monny: Amen!

CHAPTER FOURTEEN

CHANNELING

An Interview by Lady Chohan

Chohan: There seem to be many different ways of channeling. For example, there are trance mediums who allow beings from another dimension to take them over, and there are people who allow beings to talk through them and at the same time stay conscious. How I understand the way we are using channeling here, is that we are reaching for a higher level of ourselves and allowing that level to communicate with us. I wonder if you could say some things about how you see this phenomenon of channeling?

Paul: Let me start with something more general. I see the phenomenon of what we call channeling to be the pivot point of consciousness on this planet. I see it to be a medium to help people wake up. Up to now, most of the saviors have been on the outside. The saviors have been telling people that it's on the inside, but they've been listening to the savior on the outside and not to the one on the inside. With this new phenomenona that's happening, it's starting to move inside. But still, with the channeling that you're talking about, it's somebody else coming through and in a way, that's still on the outside. What we've been doing here is to start to connect with another dimension that is more personal.

The channeling you're talking about, when somebody takes over and the person stays conscious, is still only a way of describing something that as yet we don't know how to describe. It's not that. It looks like that but it's not. And then it's which level to talk about it on. At the ultimate, there is only One, you cannot channel somebody else because there isn't a somebody else, there is only the One.

Which part of that One do we tune into? What we are used to doing with our brain is talking about "this" as somebody else. Nothing is somebody else or anything else, there is only One. Then we put that into formats we can deal with, so we have the Jesuses and the Buddhas, the ascended masters and so on. They are in one category. A second category is people who can wander around but are not in a body, and a third is beings in bodies like us. They are convenient for a way of looking at things but have nothing to do with reality.

This system (points to Chohan) contains everything there is to contain, in a way that the mind can't understand. It contains the stars, it contains the planets, it contains the galaxies. It contains everything, although on another level containing isn't correct, because nothing can be contained.

"Thou art that." We've heard that over and over again. Now if it helps to say it's somebody else, that's fine. But it must be temporary, because what it's doing is very subtly saying again that it is out there, it can happen out there but it can't happen in here. What we're moving towards is saying you don't need anybody else to channel for you. You don't need anybody else to tell you anything, because everything you need to know can come through your own system. It doesn't matter whether you call it an ascended master, a higher Self, a guide, the universal consciousness or the akashic records. Every one can bring that dimension in a way that can be heard in this plane.

Chohan: When you say that, I get very excited and it seems that the view that you are presenting is very empowering. When I think of channeling another entity, there is a certain excitement in that, or a certain awe, but I see I'm also giving my power away. If you see channeling as a stepping stone that we're engaged in right now, what's after that, what's the next step?

Paul: I see people channeling as a step that says, "Look, something can happen that is beyond what you think is normal." This person seems to disappear and another takes over and says things that this one couldn't possibly know. For example, Edgar Cayce was giving medical cures that medical science didn't know anything about until years later, and he knew nothing about medical science. So people are saying, "Something is happening beyond what we can explain by our normal laws."

What's beyond that is this: as I was saying, everything that is available on any level is here. Not available here. Not can be brought through to here. Here. There is no time and there is no space. It is now.

What we call the past, what we call the future, is now. When we start to allow that possibility, there are no excuses. I don't have to come to you and listen to you telling me what I need to do. That's been our trick. What we have done is go to a channeler and if we like what we hear, we do it. If we don't like it, we say, "Well, what does this person know anyway?" We are always in control.

What is happening to the planet now is that the experiment that we undertook in this dimension of duality is over, it's finished, and we are going to dissolve the experiment. The experiment has been to disconnect from other levels of reality so that we can be totally involved in this one as if it were the only level, so we cut ourselves off. What we are going to do is uncut ourselves off.

Providing it has finished the things it needs to complete, this entity is going to be able to sit, become more quiet, listen and start to hear. In what we would call inside, there are different levels and they all have a voice, although some of them have no words. They all have a level of reality, levels and levels and levels of reality. What is going to happen with some people, is that they are going to refine themselves, purify themselves physically, in what they eat, where they live, what they think, what they do, to such a point that the level of vibration gets much finer. As it does, it starts to realize that these other levels of reality are all available, and as we fine tune ourselves, we'll be available to the next one, and the next one. Eventually, this entity will be aware of living in many dimensions, all of which have their own complete reality, at the same time.

At the moment, if all those come through together, it would just scramble you, because it would be like turning on the radio, and every station coming through at the same time. What you are going to be able to do, is have all those levels open and available, and be able to chose which one you are in, and then, when appropriate, move from one to another. In that way, you are going to be a luminous being. People are going to see that luminosity around you. They are going to know that you are the being who is in the body.

You are just here, you are not attached anymore. Any moment, you can go to another level. Going to another level is attained by stopping holding this one. Any small desire and you are back down to another level.

Chohan: I actually see what you are talking about. It's as though a doorway opens and I have a glimpse of something very immense. In the light of that vision channeling seems very gross, it seems like a childish game. If I tune into these other levels, I see that we are moving into places where telepathy and these other very fine dimensions will become normal. It may be that channeling as we speak about it in this perspective may be purely energy or a vibration rather than speaking in words which seems so clumsy from where I'm seeing it at the moment.

Paul: Think back to the Wright brothers taking their first flight and then imagine a F–16 fighter plane. Then think of a place where travel will be at the slightest desire. "I want to be in Australia." And you're there. No time, you are there. No time, no space, you just interchange between those dimensions at the slightest desire.

Chohan: Living the way we do on this planet seems pretty crude by comparison.

Paul: When you say it's crude, that's right. This dimension is very crude. On some levels, it's one of the most beautiful planets, but it's also very gross. I was looking at the cat, so beautiful, so graceful, but it's a killer and that's not beautiful. We are all killing. Russia and America spending twenty–five percent or whatever it is, of their gross national product, getting ready to kill each other.

Then people are saying, "This is awful." And they are going on peace marches to protest.

Then, if you go into the organization of peace marches, you'll find the competition is going on there, that there is a war going on within these organizations. If you go back to where they work, you'll find there is a war going on in their offices. If you look at their families, you'll find there is a war going on there. The whole point is, there is a war going on within each person, each moment. Each one of us is fighting himself, until we come to that place of acceptance, and then love. As soon as that happens, the war has ceased around us, and then wherever we go we are taking peace with us.

Chohan: In a way, what you are describing is what channeling could be if we could all manifest our divinity. If we could allow that process, then we would already be changing life around us.

Paul: As soon as the mind accepts the possibility of something outside of itself, then everything changes. The mind will never accept it, but it will accept the possibility. It can't accept it because it is not within its dimension. Once our being starts to see that, then everything stops. There's a deep breath, and suddenly we realize everything is much different than we think it is. Then comes a great respect, a great awe and, if you keep going, it becomes very normal.

Chohan: When you talk about the mind, I'm reminded that there are many people who would have very reasonable criticisms against channeling because it doesn't fit in with any rational framework that we've been conditioned to understand. It seems that the mind is the greatest barrier to this process that many of us are experiencing.

Paul: You talk about the mind as though it's a separate entity. We are totally in control of this system every moment. If we don't want the mind to think that way, it cannot. What we have done is give it a lot of space so it runs on its own, but if we don't want it to do that, it won't. When you talk about the mind not accepting, it's people who don't accept. They don't want to accept because if they did, then they'd have to look at the whole of their lives again.

Historically, people who channeled or spoke in tongues were killed for telling what everybody now knows is true. That's not going to happen this time, because in the past the planet was left on its own to do what it needed to do, and getting killed was part of the experiment. Being persecuted for what you were doing developed an experience that fed the rest of the universe.

The experiment of that learning process is over, and now it is being withdrawn in a way that people are going to have to see, one way or another. If they keep open minds, they'll be excited that all these dimensions are available because it means that we are not supreme, which is actually a rather childish belief.

Chohan: One of the things that channeling is bringing us is a sense that there are other beings outside of our known reality and that they are here to help us. That to me is a very beautiful feeling.

Paul: It's a very beautiful feeling for you, but for most people it's not, because they feel that something is greater than them and has more power than they do. This planet has been about survival and each system will kill to survive. On a very obvious level, nations kill nations, but if we really look through our layers, we're killing each other in some way or other continually.

It wants to be supreme, so when it sees something outside of itself that it cannot control, it's very threatened by that. What you're talking about is exciting to you because you've opened, because you have had a realization, you're seeing something different. If you don't have that realization, if you don't see that, it's very threatening to have something outside.

But things are happening in such a way that they cannot be denied anymore. For example, take the book, Heading Towards Omega, in which the author has collected indisputable documents to show that people have had near death experiences which have been confirmed by medical science. People have clinically died and then come back and given reports of light and love and responsibility. People from all over the world, educated and uneducated, all come back with a very similar experience.

I'm not saying this is the only experience of dying. It isn't. These people are in a certain level of consciousness. Other people who die will go to that place and have totally different experiences. Some have unpleasant experiences and others have much higher vibrations.

People are going to have to look. There is something else and this something else is not dual, it's love, pure love. It's pure acceptance, it's pure support and, if we tune into that, that's available for us, every moment. If we just disconnect from these things that keep pulling us away, if we just come here and sit and listen, it's there and it's there in every single person. There are no excuses.

You don't need to give up everything, become an atheist, join a cult or a movement or a church or anything else. You don't need anything, it's already there. If you go to somebody who already realized that and is vibrating in that energy, it will be easier. You'll get the feeling from them. You'll see that it can be done because you'll see the way they live. You'll see their grace and their beauty and you'll feel it. It will be an encouragement, but you don't need them. You don't need anything or anybody. Everything that's available in all the universes is there and there and there and there and everywhere.

CHAPTER FIFTEEN

LIVING CONSCIOUSLY

An Interview by Monny Curzon

Monny: One can get lost looking in your eyes, but one mustn't get lost and stop there.

Paul: When I look at you I feel love.

Monny: That is what's so manifest around here, with everybody who is around you. Such a collection of people, heaven knows how, and what I wonder is how this remarkable achievement will relate to the world outside. All the people we can see on the ski slopes out of the window, all the people all over the place who don't think of us and we don't think of them much. How do you see your work relating to the outside world?

Paul: I have a memory that I had many times as a child, seeing things in such a mess, the whole world in a mess, seeing people fighting each other, being upset, being angry, being anguished, hearing about the wars and the violence and the cruelty. I used to wonder how it could ever change, and then I would question whether if it was supposed to be like this. Even as a child I looked at what I could change. At that time I thought a great political leader, somebody who was in his heart and who really cared for people could do it, but every time I looked, I saw it was hopeless. I slowly realized that the only way to change the planet was if each person changed. It's no good telling people to do things that they don't want to do. If it's strange or it's difficult for them, they will not do it.

It has to happen from the inside, they have to want to do it. It's no good telling somebody not to hurt someone else because that's so obvious, that person has to realize it for himself. Then, I went through a time of hopelessness and thinking that it's impossible. I looked for ways to make a little difference, and that's why I went to Africa to work with people who were starving. I saw that I was doing a little bit, but the main problem was in the so–called civilized world.

I eventually got drawn there through the humanistic movement and started to work with people I wanted to work with. As something opened in me, I wanted to show other people that it was possible for them. Then I saw that the only way to affect anything on the larger scale was for each individual to wake up to who they are, to realize the love that is already there in them. There is love in everybody, even in the torturer or murderer. That supreme energy that has been called God is in each person. It is always there, it's just been covered up.

So I'm not looking to change the world with what I'm doing here, which is helping people who want to be helped to see themselves more clearly and see the God in them.

That has happened for you in these last two weeks and has made this whole project worthwhile to me already. You are starting to wake up to your own beauty and when you do that, other people also really start appreciating you. You are going to change, and whoever you come in contact with will see a glimpse of that love. You have started already. People can already see that love in you and now you're starting to shine with it. You're going to affect people around you and they can then catch it from you. Then they in turn start to affect the people around them and it spreads more and more. There's the possibility that all these predictions we've been having in the Bible and from Nostradamus will come true, and things will get more difficult on the planet. Then more people are going to start looking. We are now training a small team to go out and share, and eventually there will be a team of what I call shining people who have realized how beautiful they are. These people can then be in front of a television camera and they can be seen by millions. Just seeing normal people like you and I who have reached this shining place will be an encouragement for the world, and it can be an inspiration to so many people if things get bad on the planet. They'll start to see that if we can do it, then they can too. It will give them hope and they will start to look for themselves.

Monny: I can see how that could and should happen at the individual level but I worry about how it will happen on an organizational, political level. There's a great tradition of communities beginning with the highest principles and the highest people and coming more or less to sticky ends. Perhaps there's no need to think about that, but how do you imagine coping with the misapprehensions of the outside world?

Paul: That is a possibility and that possibility doesn't daunt me from being here now, because what I'm doing now is not for then. What I'm doing now is for now. What I'm doing now for me is the only thing for me to do. This is what I want to do and this is the way I want to do it. It's not for anyone else. That's what I'm suggesting to the group, not to do anything to become a shining being, although that will probably happen, just be here as who you are now. If you're not enjoying yourself now, you probably won't enjoy yourself then. It's learning to really be doing what you want to be doing in each moment.

It's true that there is a tradition of such communities going off the rails, but before that a long time ago there was a period where that didn't happen. Then there were shining communities where everybody was working in love and caring, and light.

There's a critical mass. There is a time when enough people, and it doesn't have to be the majority of people but the majority of energy, reach a certain point and then it starts to affect everybody and everything starts to move that way. One of the reasons that spiritual communes and other communities that are looking for what is called a higher way of living have gone off in the past is their structure. The leader has it and the rest don't. Now, I know that is not true, every single person has that shining place within himself.

What's happening here is not an organization where one person has woken up and says to everybody, "Follow this." Here one person has started to wake up and has said, "Now you start to wake up. And as you start to wake up, be your authority and don't listen to anybody else as an authority. Wake up and start to take responsibility for yourself. Continue to listen to other people, but always take responsibility for yourself."

Of course, there will be a type of pyramid, but instead of there being just one person who is awake, the idea is that many people start to awaken. In the traditional therapy circles, one leader has worked on his own because there has always been the therapist there, there's been one strong person and then lesser people around. Then, even when Jung and Freud were working, as soon as they came to a certain strength, they split off from the leader and started a little group of their own.

What's happening here is something very different. Here we have a group of very powerful, very accomplished, mature people who are at different levels which are constantly changing, moment to moment, as they wake up. So, instead of being one leader, there are many, and there are going to be more and more working as a team. This is unusual because, normally, strong people still have an ego and therefore they can't work together. What's happening here is a bunch of people are really looking at that competitive part of themselves, that part that wants to rule on its own, and they're letting it go so we can have a team. The team is going to become bigger and bigger but we're not going to have an organization.

Already there are different centers and small communities starting, but they have nothing to do with this except in a heart connection. They're all autonomous and they're encouraged to do the same thing they're doing here when they go out in the world. Have one person who has the ultimate responsibility, who has the overall view, but keep giving the responsibility away and don't have "a leader."

Monny: That certainly sounds radically different from the traditional, hierarchical, vertical communities that one has heard about. Intellectually, it's much more exciting because it is the moon to the sun I suppose. I wonder, however, about the world beyond that. We've talked about evil before. Malice may be an easier term than evil. How will you cope with that?

Paul: I don't think we will cope with it directly because we're not directly concerned with it. We're not interested in changing anybody who doesn't want to change. We're not out to save the world unless the world wants to be saved, and when we talk about the world or we talk about malice, we're talking about something generally.

Generally, I don't look at things generally! I look at the individual and see what the person wants, what he is available for. And people need to ask for that because I don't feel any drive or any urge in me to change people who don't want to change. If they're unconscious and it looks like they want to be unconscious, that's fine. If they get a glimpse or they hear or they see something on the television, and they get something that says, "Well, what is that? I'd like to look at that." Then I feel open to sharing something with them. But I'm not going to interfere in the government and organizations. I'm not interested in situations where people are not interested in themselves.

Monny: May they not interfere with you? Governments are not averse to interference.

Paul: What I feel is that a government will interfere when it feels threatened, when somebody is aggressive towards it. Then it's difficult to explain, but on an energy level I've seen it happen. I've come up to borders where people are having their cars searched and are getting angry and upset. What I see is the custom official just doing his job and I don't feel any aggression towards him. I don't get upset, even if he does ask me to get out of my car in the rain and open the trunk. Usually, what happens is he just waves me on because I'm not upset with him.

When you talk about the possibility of evil or malice, it is something that resides within the mind of man. It's something we have produced in this dimension and we were meant to produce it. We decided to do that because the only way of appreciating life was to dichotomize it, and thus see its opposite. We have now reached the extreme of that and my feeling is we're starting to come back.

I feel that it is starting to happen with the Russian leader and with some other powerful people. I know it is not happening everywhere yet, but something is starting. Something is moving to its extreme and as it does, so the love grows stronger too. There are more people meditating now, more people looking for their higher Selves or reading spiritual books and more people searching for something more out of their lives than there have ever been.

Monny: That is the positive side. But there's also the suggestion that there's more fear and that fear, if aroused, if crystallized, is deadly.

Paul: Fear has a turning point. It can move either into violence or into love, because fear is actually the opposite of love. It is actually the same frequency as excitement. It works on the same vibration and if there's a "no" to it, it goes into fear. If there's a "yes," it goes into excitement, into a possibility. Many people are starting to see that there is a new possibility that life doesn't have to be the old way. It could still go the old way and to me, it doesn't matter which way it goes, because I'm not out to change anything.

There is an awakening in me. I can see. I am seeing things in a different way and I can see that other people can see that too. Something has happened inside me and I can see that it can happen in each person. It's fun to share that with people who want to share it, and for the people who don't, that's okay too.

Monny: Compared to that, nothing is terribly interesting. Can enough people feel that, glimpse that?

Paul: Because of their affluence, a lot of people are seeing that what used to be exciting for them – obtaining a certain amount of money, or prestige or possessions – doesn't work anymore. Then, from the conditioning they've had, there isn't anything else. Maybe there's something vaguely religious, but it has not been an inspiration in the recent past because people who have been in that study themselves have never reached a place that's been encouraging.

Some people are starting to wake up and they are starting to see there is something else to achieve and it's beginning to excite them. It's not really in fashion at the moment, but eventually there are going to be other famous people like Shirley Maclaine who are going to declare, "This is the most interesting thing in my life now. I've had glimpses of other dimensions and other worlds that exist now. I've seen that for myself. I know that." They are people who are being given so much credence, that when they say, "I know that," people are going to listen and say, "Well if that's so, then I'm going to investigate this for myself."

When they see normal people like you and me, not people who have been born of virgin mothers, starting to reach a place of love and caring and genuine compassion, something will open in them. They are going to be interested, because the old way isn't working and somewhere we all know that.

Monny: There is a valued tradition, in the West as well as the East, of people going into a monastery and looking for a life of contemplation and meditation, after having achieved significant worldly success, and I can imagine that coming back.

You speak of yourself as an ordinary person and that's true, but often you talk of things which are highly extraordinary and esoteric and that sets my alarm bells going, as you know. What it would set going in other people out in the world, I shudder to think. Is it not important to be very careful, step by step by step going over these steps you've forgotten below you?

Paul: There are two things here. First there is a tradition in the West of a few people going into monasteries, but really there is very little encouragement for anybody to go into the monastery. It's normally very serious, very unpleasant and nobody shines out of there, nobody comes flying out of there and says, "Everybody, you must do this. It's fantastic!" In our recent past, there's been no encouragement. I think what's going to happen is people are going to wake up and they're going to shine, and they're not going to have to go into a monastery. They're going to be able to do it in the world, maybe in a slightly protected environment, in small communities, but they're not going to hide themselves away and do something that I consider is not part of being human. I'm looking for people to be in the world in a natural way, doing it in their families, while they're in their relationships, while they are working, doing it while including everything.

The other thing is you talk about "the gap," and that's true. As I have started to awaken, I've tried to stop myself going too fast, because as I start to awaken to this and see these other dimensions, I can feel the gap to the person that still thinks these things "esoteric." As they happen, they are very ordinary. As you start to see these other levels or dimensions, you know that you've seen them all the time. It's very hard to explain, but you know that you've always known, but you didn't recognize it. As my system becomes more sensitive and starts to move more into these realms, I know it starts to widen this gap. What I've looked to do with myself is to be at a pace where there's always somebody following very closely and that's what the inner team has been. As I move, they move.

We then have another step to the trainees and then behind the trainees, at the moment, are the participants of this group. So, when I come out and talk, I know a lot of the participants say, "Well, what's he talking about? It's too far away, it's a dream, it's science fiction." But then the trainers come and they talk, and it's not so far away. My feeling is that this is going to build and build and there's always going to be some sort of connection, because these levels of consciousness exist around us in this space. Even some scientists have either glimpsed or understood this now. There is no space and there is no time. It's a concept, it's a way of looking at things. It's the mind's way of dealing with something, but there is no space and there is no time. All space is contained here and now, right in this moment. Then, there is an awakening on this planet and there are forces to help us awaken.

Now some entities, consciousnesses, beings, have decided to come as close as they possibly can to this dimension without being in a body, and others have decided to come in bodies. The ones who are out of bodies get channeled so people go into certain states and start to talk in strange voices, in strange ways, but what they say is very powerful. It is the stuff that's been written in the holy books. But it doesn't touch the human so closely as a Jesus or a Buddha who took a body to say these things and to reach the same places of consciousness. By saying their message from a body they can make this connection more strongly, because they understand, because they've been through the birth process. They've been through childhood and school so they understand that.

But as you say, the more refined the energy, the less they can connect with the human. Here the trainees are in contact with the participants. There is a definite connection there. The trainees are fully in contact with the ones who have been trained. There's a connection there. The trained ones are fully in contact with me, so there is a connection all the way through. Although there's this connection, I keep reminding you that you don't need it. The Kingdom of God is literally within. Everything is contained there.

Monny: One thing that's evident is that you're having a lot of fun and joy. There's a spirit, a joy around you, around those close to you and it spreads like wildfire in our group of people who come from all over the place and that obviously is highly contagious and...delightful. Yet, people who have not seen you and seen the people here, will read things that you send out and think this is very odd, very suspect. People must, at best, think we are all slightly batty. It's to delay the onset of their rejection that's the direction of my inquiry. I think it should be delayed, because those people are very important and have a lot to contribute.

Paul: Let's take what you said about spreading like wildfire. That is the way it will work. What took several weeks and maybe months to obtain in the last course we reached here in a few days, because a number of the people who were in the six–month course have come here as trainees and they've brought their energy and the participants have caught it very quickly. So that is the method, if it can be called a method, that we are using. We are not using any traditional methods, the techniques are just subsidiary. You just catch it.

The next thing I'll talk about is that we're having fun. If we're not, then I don't know what we're doing. In a way, the main thing is that we're enjoying what we're doing now, not planning what we are going to do or how we are going to be in the future. That is all secondary. The main thing is having fun.

I think that's been a drawback for many of the schools in the past. When you look at what you have to go through to get to where they're saying you can get to, it looks so miserable that it's very deterring. In a way, we are saying that to have fun is the most important thing. As soon as we get too serious, we'll stop the spiritual growth. If that happens, we need to stop everything because something went off the rails.

The next thing is the people who hear about us but don't actually know about us. Within the system is this place you call malice, or evil, or we could just call it cynicism or negativity. It gets triggered so easily in people because that's the direction in which the planet has gone for many years. That has been the main energy, to doubt, pull it down, say it's not true. Mostly, it hasn't been true.

We are not concerned with these people. I'm not saying we don't care. Concern says, "You have to change so I can feel better." We care, which means, "We would like you to see what we're seeing, if that's what you'd like, but if you don't, it doesn't affect how we feel. Our happiness is not geared to your approval."

When people read things, then of course, the cynicism comes up because they don't feel the energy. It is impossible for us to say in words what's happening here and you'll see that when you go back out and someone asks you, "What's happened?" You look, nothing happened, there's nothing you can explain, except we had a good time and you went through a few uncomfortable moments. It's very hard to explain.

We are getting messages from other dimensions. That's a fact. It's as much a fact to some people as feeling this floor under your feet. A few people here do channeling at the computer. They're sitting there and these words are flowing through them, things they couldn't possibly say to themselves, things they don't know anything about. At times they doubt what is happening, but the fact is the information keeps coming through. There's somebody here who channeled a whole design for an energy sphere to build up energy. He didn't know what was happening while he was doing it. Information was coming through that he didn't know anything about. Even while it was coming through, part of him was still skeptical, saying, "What's this?" or "Where's this coming from? Am I making it up?" In each person there's that skeptical part. Now, if you keep supporting that negative part, that doubter, you'll never know. All you do is stay in the known. You have to say "Look, I don't know if this is true or not, but I'm going to take it as a hypothesis for a while." Then it starts to become true and then what can you say? It's your truth.

Monny: What I'd like to see more of is that form of creative doubt that you speak of that the person had. That immediately feels healthy, and not skeptical knocking.

Paul: It's what I call a floating doubt and everybody needs that. A floating doubt says, "I do not know what the truth is because nobody knows what the truth is. There is a place that's called enlightenment where the person is supposed to know what the truth is, but I don't know whether that's true or not. I suppose I won't know until I'm there." So, we don't know. That's a fact, and if you look around at our society, we all know we don't know.

At the moment, we still have surgeons cutting people open and taking organs out. At the same time, we have people who can just put their hands on the body and do the same thing, and this has been documented scientifically and is proved beyond doubt. We don't know.

If we can dare to move through that place, especially men, to a place that doesn't know, and doubt everything, then we are on the way home. Then you say, "So, I hear that somebody can channel another entity...or that there's another level of consciousness within this one. I don't know whether that's true or not. I'll go and find out." That's what I call a healthy doubt.

From what I hear, that's what Russia is doing. If somebody has a psychic ability, instead of trying to prove it scientifically, which means using the old methods, they say, "You can obviously do something that I can't. Now, if you can do it, the possibility is that I can do it." Not trying to prove it in a formula, or scientifically, but saying, "It is happening." So if Yuri Geller can bend metal without touching it, it's a possibility that other people can too. Let's play with it, let's see who can do it. That sounds healthy to me.

Monny: And it sounds more acceptable to this male mind if it can be invited to play with these concepts, not confronted with a whole lot of things that will bring up instant projection. After all, the male mind is part of us like our teeth. You can't throw your food into your stomach in one good chew. The intellect is great for chewing.

Paul: There is something there. I've heard that if somebody is very skeptical and very negative, then Yuri Geller can't do those things. There is a level of vibration that is affected by a person who is very negative, and then they won't happen. When you say that you can't throw it right through, in fact, that is the only way.

The mind, as we know it, is actually a block. The mind, again scientifically, activates through the left hand side of the brain, which is like a mechanical side, whereas the right hand side of the brain, we're talking about the brain, not the mind, is the receptive side, is the intuitive side. In fact, when it sees things that impurely, then going through the purely mechanical side, it is like a computer. It gets programmed and it's very fixed, and therefore anything new has great difficulty reaching the being, which is not the mind. So, this mind stops things with the old and tries to prove it in the old way, and the other side of the brain, the right hand side of the brain which is intuitive, which is actually in connection with these higher levels, usually is fed that way. What many of the schools are trying to do is say, "Look, you need that, you need that to know your name, but put it on the side for a moment and see if you can receive things directly without chewing, without the teeth. See if you can just take it in."

That's the way the female side works and that is what's often the cause of friction between the male and the female because often the female says, "Oh, I know that." And the male says, "How can you know that? I haven't even told you the details yet." And she says, "I know that." She just took the whole thing in and she got it, whereas the male works through things bit by bit, and that's often where the conflict is between the man and the woman. They work in different ways. The woman can get it. The phone can ring and she can say, "Oh that's auntie so and so." And the man can say, "Oh, you can't possibly know that." But she does, because she received it in another way, through another vibration. That's what the male part of the mind doesn't understand. It can't work that way.

Again, it is a fact that most of the inventions, most of the leaps that have happened, have not happened through the drawing board or through calculation. The drawing board and the calculation are the preparation, but usually the idea came in a sweep or a flash or in the bath or, "Yes! That's it!" It didn't work its way through, it didn't go through the male part of the mind. It flashed into the female part of the mind and suddenly they knew. Then, having known it, they could go back and work out the details and make it functional and useful.

Monny: Perhaps, if they hadn't had male minds, they might have been assailed with nonsensical flashes, any sort of irrational twaddle that is floating around.

Paul: Even if it isn't irrational twaddle, they would have flashes that they wouldn't be able to interpret, that would be useful on this plane. So, it's like you would get a new program for your computer, but you couldn't read it and then the male mind reads it. So often, the female gets something and she has something, but it's not practical and it takes the male to make it practical. But what we've done in the past is, we've put these two up against each other. "This is right and this is wrong."

Generally, on this planet, the male has to slow down a bit and the female has to be given a bit more encouragement. We're afraid to do that because the female side is very, very powerful, and then the male thinks it's going to lose its control. What's needed is a cooperation, a balance among us all. We have to have the courage to go to a place that we haven't had the courage to go to in the past.

There is evidence that there have been societies where the woman has been in charge, and that didn't work. Now we have a society where the male is in charge and that doesn't work either. We have to get to this place where we start to make a balance and where we start to cooperate and go into all those uncomfortable places in ourselves. From that, we produce this balance that is love, that is caring. And then the male can function in true harmony with the female.

CHAPTER SIXTEEN

MEDITATION

An Interview by Phoenicia Graham

Phoenicia: I've listened to and read a lot about meditation and there seem to be many different ideas about what it is. Yet, I've always had the feeling that at the source there is one central feeling which is meditation, or one central beingness which is meditation, and everything else has been a build up to it.

Paul: The difficulty in talking about meditation is that it isn't anything and therefore you have many descriptions about something that's not. What most people do are meditation techniques, and they may lead to a place that people call meditation.

There are many techniques according to different directions and different schools going to this same place. Some of the techniques give you a mantra, which is saying over and over a particular word or sound which has a vibration. That is designed to move into your vibration and help you to come to a balanced and neutral place. Other techniques help you to follow your breath in and out.

What most of them are doing is helping you be present, because most of the time most people are not present. They think they're here, but they are not here now. There are two main techniques of meditation. One is the oriental technique, where you do a mantra, or you do something that brings you a thereness without being here, and then there's the Zen techniques, where you follow the breath and you listen to the sounds, which is another sort of here.

There was an experiment done with that in the United States that I read about, where people who reach very deep states of meditation were put into a soundproof chamber, and then had electrodes put on them to read what was happening to their systems. With the Eastern meditators from India, when a sound was made, the system would jump. When the sound was made a second time, the system would jump less, until eventually it took no notice. So the sharp sound came and the meditator was gone, had left the body and moved into other levels of consciousness. With the Zen meditator every time the sound went, the meditator jumped exactly the same.

What I see with the two types of meditation with this experiment is that one has left and gone into other realms, maybe consciously, maybe not, and the other one is here. I found that the most pure type of meditation and I'm not saying it's the most suitable or the easiest, is not doing anything but being here. That is, when you have a thought, you are aware of having the thought, when you have a feeling, you are aware of having a feeling. If you're disturbed, you're aware of being disturbed and don't do anything about it. You just watch. Then eventually the same sort of things happen, whether it comes through the Zen or the Indian type of meditation. You start to see that there are other realms to do with this realm. Within this moment, there are other moments. Within this consciousness, there are other consciousnesses. There are depths and depths, or heights and heights, whichever way you see it, of this moment. And you start to realize them.

So, some people start to see past lives, and then what happens is they lose themselves in that. They see themselves killing somebody or being killed and they're off into that situation, they've lost this moment. Or they might see themselves as their ascended Selves, as they are going to be, then they start to see their shining beings and they go off to be these, and again they lose this moment, they lose the watcher.

What I see as the most helpful is being here, and just watching. It's very difficult for a person when he starts. Down through the ages, that is the thread from all the masters, practically all of them meditate, sit. So few people do it because it's so difficult. As soon as you sit, you become aware of all those thoughts that were going on all the time, that you haven't registered. The mind is an orchestra that's not in harmony, chattering away, each instrument playing its own tune. It's chaos and the person gets discouraged.

What many of the schools say is stop the mind, and nobody knows how to do that. What they do is try to suppress it and then they feel more and more uncomfortable. What I found most useful is to just watch. You sit, close your eyes or have them half-open, look ahead, and watch the whole situation. You hear the noises outside, you can feel your mind moving, a disturbance in the body, or the emotions, and you watch. And you watch. And you watch. As you do that, the system starts to slow down.

Then another thing happens. The active part of the mind, which is generally said to be the left-hand side of the brain, starts to slow down. Normally, it's out there looking and working things out and going through all its past conditioning to see if it is safe, if it is all right. "Should I do this? Should I do that?" It's very, very active.

As you sit and watch, it starts to slow down, because there's nothing to do. You're just watching. If you get engaged in a thought, "Should I sell my shares now, or should I change my job, or do this?" Then it activates again. You see the thought go by, "Should I sell my shares now?" And it just goes by, and you don't do anything about it, you don't need that active side of the brain, so it gets slower. As it gets slower, it starts to be aware that there is a right-hand side of the brain, that normally doesn't have much say in things because it's female, it's passive, it's open, it's receptive.

This is the side that is in touch with other dimensions, in touch with all the things that have been learned throughout the universe. It is like a radio station to other dimensions, but it has no aggression, it has no pushing power. Normally, the left side of the brain never listens, it just works from a very shallow place.

As it slows down, it starts to be aware of the other side, and these two start to balance. As they balance, this side that is receiving, that is open, that is the intuition, that knows things beyond knowledge and intellect, can start feeding across the information it has. As this is slowed down, it starts to listen, and the left-hand side of the brain is the side that puts things into action. The right-hand side can't act on anything, it receives the information, passes it across, and then, from a quieter place, action can happen.

I see the most use for meditation is just to sit. Then, it is really useful to go to somebody regularly, to share with them what is going on, so they can say, "Well, I think what you forgot was..." Or, "You got lost..." Or, "What you need to look at is..." It is also very helpful to get some advice on how to hold the body in a more relaxed posture. But, it needs to be easy, not this forcing, not this seriousness, not this attaining.

Meditation is not to attain anything, it's just the opposite, it's to let go. Most people sit to attain these levels of realization, so, they are "doing" again, and that is the left-hand side of the brain out of balance. It's a passivity, it's just sitting and allowing. As Jesus and all the masters have said, "The Kingdom of God is within." Now. You don't have to develop it, it's there now. You just have to learn to listen.

Phoenicia: This links with something else I was thinking. Bankai sat for almost twenty years in an isolated and cold mountain hut on the stone floor with his knees bleeding. There was only that in his life, only sitting and watching for twenty years.

Then I look at myself, and this sounds a bit overwhelming. I have the feeling this is what you have been talking about, that it doesn't have to take twenty years, that it's not necessary for what settles through meditation to take so long.

Paul: It was actually longer than twenty years and in horrific conditions. He sat and he sat, and then he attained his liberation. His teaching was a very simple message. It was, "There was no need to do that. What I attained through that is available in you, now." With Bankai, it was not the time, it was not the conditions, it was the intent. He said, "I am going there." And that was the only way he knew, because all the masters he went to said, "You have to sit."

What he found was, with all the masters he went to except one, was that they did not know themselves, they hadn't realized. We tend to read these books and look back and think there were hundreds of enlightened people strolling all over the place. At one time there were maybe ten. Maybe that is the most there has ever been. Most of the time there weren't any. He didn't have the guidance, but he had the intent.

There are Sufi stories about people who were told by their master, "Give up this and move." Then, when they had established themselves, "Give up this and move." And when they became successful merchants and they had everything around them, the master said again, "Give this up and move." It's nothing to do with giving it up, it's the intention. Is the intention more important than what you have built around you? If it is, you don't have to move.

Phoenicia: I have been reading about people who are doing research on alternative treatments for cancer, AIDS and heart disease. What I have picked up is a thread in all of them. They all have a basis of what you could call meditation, or the inward path, involved in them. I have a feeling that in each of us there is a knowing that this is the way, that everything else is a distraction or is a death, that this is somehow the only possibility of life, of some kind of healthy beingness. And yet, when I look, who picks that up?

Paul: You know the party game where you whisper a message to your friend and then she whispers a message to the next person and so on, and then when it comes all the way back, it's not the same message that started out? We started out as beings who decided to take a body, but it was so fine that it was hardly here. Ill health was not a consideration, it just kept itself healthy. It didn't eat, it didn't drink. It was just a very gentle collection of molecules that decided to just about stay in this state, so that as part of the One we could appreciate each other and experiment with duality. It was very fine. Then it was passed on to the next one and it got a little bit more solid, and then a little bit more solid and so on and so on.

Then we grow old. There is no need to grow old, growing old is a conditioning. Other people grow old, so you think you grow old, so you grow old.

You see people who have cancer and die, so when you get cancer you think you are going to die. You see a certain number of people with illness, so you think that is a possibility and you start to create the possibility in yourself. As you sit, if you sit in this place where you become empty, you start to see and realize that every one of those cells in you, every one of those molecules in you, has a consciousness of its own, it's together by agreement. It's got locked there because of the way the story's been told. It doesn't know it's free. Now, if you sit, you start to see that, you start to see that you can heal yourself. You don't need a Jesus to do it, you don't need somebody to lay their hands on you. You can do it.

There are many documented stories of people who have been incurable. They lie down and then visualize the component that's not healthy, and the components that make up the components, and then they visualize them healthy. And they heal themselves. This is absolutely possible. If you want it as a desire, as a choice, you probably won't get it. You'll create the opposite because you contract, "I don't want to die. I don't want to be ill." That contraction stops the molecules moving, that's how you got ill in the first place. You had a resentment, you had a judgment. There are things that you didn't express, that you didn't do.

You didn't leave your job when you needed to leave it, you stayed on because of the money, because of the security. You contract. That's what makes you ill. As you sit, you start to expand, and then you start to put things right. This is a self-healing system, it doesn't want to be ill. The only reason it's ill is because you held. Start letting go and you start to heal.

Then, if you sit with enough intent, you begin to see the levels of consciousness in this moment and you'll see that one of them is already healthy, and then you choose to start to identify with that.

I've worked with a lot of people who worked with people who were dying of cancer and what all these people said is, "If the person hasn't moved to a certain state where it is too late, that cancer is curable." Most people don't cure it because they want to die. That's why they got cancer in the first place. They don't realize that, but somewhere they gave up. A lot of people have said that about AIDS too, that the person doesn't realize that, but somewhere he gave up, it was too much, he lowered his resistance and things came tumbling in. Illness is an attitude, it's a thought, it's a vibration. It got there through one attitude, one thought, one vibration. It can disappear the same way.

Phoenicia: What seems to happen to people when they first sit is they are very aware of their minds, then they come to a stage where, through sitting and sitting, the mind seems to slow down.

Then it seems to go through different stages and barriers, and there are moments when it feels as if I had never meditated at all. It's like I'm right back at the beginning. There are times when my mind goes absolutely nuts and I'm wondering if there is some kind of thread through all this. Is this the same for everyone?

Paul: Nothing is the same for everyone. There isn't an isn't. You need to find someone who has been through these levels. This is why there are masters and teachers. They know those levels themselves. Either they have done it in this life or they have woken up to their past lives, and they know they have been through it. If you go to such a person he would give you a little advice, but the main thing is he'll give you encouragement. That's all you need. There are stages, but there is no need to go through these stages. It's the intent that's important, the stages are produced by your holding.

Maybe sitting one day, you get the realization that you are in the wrong job, it's perfectly clear. We have somebody here who is in the inner team who had this when she was in Australia. She was sitting one day, and then she woke up in the morning and sat up in bed. This realization came without any doubt whatsoever, that she had to leave where she was and come and join us. That was her next step. She came out of the meditation so excited that she was getting ready to pack straight away. As the day moved on, her mind came back in and said, "Well, I've just built up a nice clientele here, I'm doing a useful job in Australia where it's needed and we've just got this house and we've got comfortable." Slowly the message started to fade away. Those stages are resistance.

One day the message might be, "Leave this boyfriend or leave this girlfriend." Then you delay it while you think about it, and produce a stage, you try to go around it. You say, "I'll do that later." Or, "What do I do now?" Doing this produces the stages. If it's a total yes, you just move and move and you are already home.

There are stages and they come at different times for different people. You can never compare yourself. So, some people may be seeing angelic forms around them and you think they are way ahead of you, but then they get stuck in the angelic forms. You have to let go of them. You have to let everything go.

Then other people feel as though they are struggling with unpleasant past lives. To some people that's an advancement, because they have never had a past-life experience. Other people will be already seeing golden angels. You can't compare. You need to come to somebody who can see and all he does is say, "It's fine."

It doesn't matter what's going on. Maybe you need a little encouragement because it's getting too much. He may say, "Try this out. Try that." You don't need to do anything, you just sit and be available, and then you start to get your message. When you do, follow it.

One of the reasons some people do not follow the messages is they see them as other entities which, in one way, they are. Others see them as their higher or their inner Selves. Often, the message is quite radical and when you come back out of this state you check the message with your mind and your mind isn't in the same state. It has no facility to check that message. Not only that, the brain is in two parts, so it can say yes to this and no to that. In this other place, there are no two parts and there was no doubt, it was just yes. Not even yes, it just was. Then you say,

"Well, I'll check that out." You can't check it out. Often, it happens more with women, because they are closer to their intuition.

We reach levels of vibrations, levels of realization and we know this is so and we come back and then we imagine our Uncle Fred or our father saying, "Prove it to me." You can't prove it and, if you try, you lose it to yourself. So it's a gamble and the ego hates that. It likes certainties.

Phoenicia: That was a question for me. I have also seen in myself that, in sitting, there is often a place which is absolutely empty and quiet. But when the forty minutes is over, I come back, I get up, I charge out of the room and I am back in the old gear again. What I am looking at in myself is integrating that quiet, that space, that stillness into this movement and this action all through the day.

Paul: First of all, let's appreciate sitting. If you have been sitting for forty minutes and you have become still, you are healing yourself on every level. You are healing the body, the emotions and the mind. When you get up and move around, you'll have a different quality to people who don't sit. You can tell the people who meditate as soon as you meet them. There is something else around them, something different is happening to them. So, first of all, appreciate what happens in that state.

The second thing is, that's the game. It's no good just having it during your forty minutes. It has to become every second of your twenty-four hours. For that you need to slow down a little bit. If you dash off, you are going to make it more difficult for that connection. Just come back a little more slowly. As you talk to somebody, be a little more aware, be a little slower, a little more present, a little more available. Then you'll start to feel the things that have happened in those forty minutes have got the space to slide through.

We can look at it like the two sides of the brain again, that they become balanced, they come into harmony. They are working with each other. This side has the concept and the other side puts it into action. You wake up and this becomes so active, you are out of touch with this again. Slow down so that you start to move across.

When you are with somebody, be with them. When you look at somebody, look at them. When you are sitting in the chair, feel yourself sitting on the chair. Hear the sounds. Expand and you'll slow down automatically, and eventually you'll start to see that there are many dimensions stacked in the same dimension.

Yes, this is an aggressive person who is attacking you, and beneath, there is a very frightened person who is having to attack because he is afraid you are going to attack him. Beneath that is a very loving person, beneath that, and beneath that... there is God. In everybody.

But to appreciate that, you have to slow down, and you have to keep yourself on the move. This system, as a system, keeps trying to survive in an animalistic way. It keeps trying to build its den, its nest, its relationship, its money, its appreciation and fame, and then hold it. Then you are stuck, you've got to let it go, and let it go. And it's part of the process, why we've moved out of our Villa in Italy. It was one of the most beautiful places in the world, going very successfully, people wanting to come, everything going perfectly, but everything was becoming a little sleepy. It was getting a little settled. As you know, that is what we do. We used to move rooms every now and again, but now we are moving countries. The people who were getting comfortable are saying, "Look, it's beautiful what we have learned." But the truth is that it's useless to you unless you know how to be that in the world. Go back out into the world and start to feel that and practice it there. That does two things, it takes what you have learned deeper, and it also helps other people, because they start to see what has happened, and it gives them hope. It gives them encouragement to go on, to look for a quieter place in themselves.

Phoenicia: My last question has to do with the path of meditation, and I want to go back to the idea of the picture of Bankai. When I look at that, it seems to me that Bankai's path was meditation and when I look at us as a team of people, as a group of people being together, it looks to me like meditation is a part of our path. Somehow, the way we are moving is bigger than that.

Paul: That's right and at the same time it's not right. Our path is meditation. It's just that its form is different. What Bankai did, and what the Buddhist path generally is, is negation. That is, they got born into this planet, they decided to be here and then they decide to negate it. Not this, not that, not anything, no God, no self, nothing.

And it's been successful in the past but I find it ugly. I find the whole concept of Buddhism ugly. He was a very beautiful man from what I have read, and many beautiful things happened around him, but it's all "no." He is quoted as saying, "A woman is a bag of skin full of filth." What I'm saying is, include everything. You came here, this is part of everything. Why come here and then negate it? Why call it ugly? Why call it separate? Nothing is separate. Come here, and be part of everything, and include everything and find this place within you. In one way, even though Bankai sat for twenty odd years on a stone, bleeding and starving, that was the easiest way for him. He cut himself off and found it in isolation. Then, when he came to teach, he never really connected with people because the people who came to him weren't of that same intent. They weren't of that same commitment. He found it by his isolation, and it's the same with many other masters. In one way, it's the same with Krishnamurti. He found it, but he found it in such an artificial way, he could never really connect. He didn't connect with people who are sexual, because he hadn't been through that part in himself.

I remember, when I used to follow motor racing, my hero was Stirling Moss. He never had the latest car because if he had had, he always would have won. He used to have last year's car because he raced for a private company that never had the latest model. And then the fun for him was, could he still win?

Give yourself a handicap. Can you win? What I'm saying is, be in the world, have all the temptations, go into your sex, and can you still hold that place? Because if you can't, it's not real. You get in an artificial situation and then, when you come out, you may still have it, but you are cut off.

I am talking about expanding and finding that place, whatever we want to call it, meditation, knowing, the stillness, the peace that passeth all understanding. Finding that place and being in the world.

CHAPTER SEVENTEEN

THE ART OF SEEING

An Interview by Velusia

Velusia: Having worked with you for so many years, I have had the close opportunity to see how you have changed the way you relate to people when you are working with them. I was remembering yesterday how incredibly touched I always was with the heart space with which you connected to people. In the last year, I have noticed this connecting process becoming much less personal, though the effect that it's having on people is just as strong. How do you find that process in yourself?

Paul: When somebody asked me a question with a certain intensity, it was like a switch was thrown inside me. Something clicked and another vibrational state of being opened. It has very much to do with the person who asks the question. It's almost like being the person, and in this click a certain state happens and information comes through. What developed in me was a way that I could see people so that I could see their past traumas, in this life and other lives.

Then I found that something wanted to go on developing in me and I didn't want to stay in that state. I could see, but to do that I had to come down, and I wanted to go on going up. Then I had to make the decision whether I was going to go on using this talent that could see people and connect with them in a heart space.

It was a great gift, a great skill, and it developed to a finer and finer level, until almost as soon as the person sat down, even before they asked the question, the click would happen and I would be ready. Then I found I was restless with that. It was as though it was holding me down, and my mind couldn't understand that because I had spent my whole life devoted to developing this talent.

To read people's thoughts and pasts like a book was what I had wanted. The thought of letting that go, or not even using it, seemed somehow a travesty, as though I was given a gift and I was putting it in the cupboard and not using it. There was a period when we were working together, when I kept saying, "I don't want to go in that group room. I don't want to talk to these people." I couldn't understand that, because as soon as I sat down, all that disappeared and the talent started to happen in the old way. But this restlessness remained, so I decided to give space to it. Then, a lot of this facility started to fade, it was still there but if I wanted it I had to make an effort to bring it back, and in the process I came down in vibration. Getting to a facility that had taken me my whole life to produce, brought me down. Then what happened was, the energy started moving upwards. It became finer, and in the process, it became less personal, about me, my life, my likes, dislikes and wants.

Then another level of seeing myself opened in me, and I could then see that level in other people, but they couldn't see it themselves.

What I feel now, in some strange way, is that I love the person more than in the old way, but it is not an emotional loving, it's like a cool loving. I love the higher part of the person that they don't even know is there. I talk about it, I talk about the ascended Self, I talk about the light that is always there, but nobody knows what I am talking about. They say to themselves, "Oh yes, that's a possibility. I think I know what he is talking about. I had that in meditation. I had that on an acid trip." Often, when I am suggesting this and that, the other person's higher Self says, "That's right, that's what I have been telling him all the time. I have been trying to get that message through. Go on, tell him." The higher Self is this person who is awake in there, but it can't get through to the lower self because the lower self is so involved in the personal, the character and the lower levels.

What I used to do was to go down to the lower levels, get inside the person and then try and move him up, and say "Look at this, how do you feel about this? Go and try that and come back." Now I can't do that without contaminating my own system, and that is one of the reasons why I am so intensely training the people around me, so they can fill in those places. What I usually say is, "This is living in this space, this is my reality. Now, see if you can catch that. You can't understand it, but see if you can catch it." When the person opens unconditionally, he is not disagreeing with me and he is not agreeing with me, those are to do with the lower self. He is just saying, "I don't know and I want to know." The fewer conditions that are there, the sooner the system starts to open, and then he feels this vibrating. As he feels this, he realizes it is not me he is feeling, it's that level of vibration that is in him. Then, for that moment, he looks down at his problems and difficulties and just laughs. He might go away and get caught in his relationships or his money and forget, but he knows that higher place is there.

Velusia: It seems as though, when they connect with you on this new level, they are bypassing their emotions or their hearts, and for a while that seems very confusing. It's as though we have learned to relate to the vulnerability of being touched in the heart space, even though that shakes us and makes us vulnerable. It seems that where you are relating from now is somewhere beyond that.

Paul: What often happens is things get dichotomized and people say you have got to work through every single thing, you can't bypass anything, everything has to be experienced and karma has to be paid. Then there is another school, which says just jump to this higher level and it is all over. Neither of them is true. If you work on these lower levels, on the problems and catharsis and the resentment, you have a lot of working out to do for this lifetime. Then, when you have done that, you have to go through the birth trauma, and then through the conception and the death in your last life. After that you have to work through the previous life. It's endless. You can't do that. It's impossible because all the time you are doing that, you are building up more trauma in this moment. You are so busy in the past that you are unconscious in the present, and then you have got to deal with that in what you call the future.

The other side says, "Just jump and you are clear." In one way that is true, but there are very few people who are able to make such a big jump. Most people need to make a certain jump and then they move into this new level of vibration. Then they need to deal with these things that need to be dealt with, but from this new level, not from the old one. If you deal with problems on the level of a problem, you are just spinning problems. If you flip to this other level and just say, "Yes, I can't avoid that, I have to go through that," you are in a different vibration. It goes very quickly when you approach it that way.

Velusia: I was wondering if there isn't a danger, when you are working with people in an impersonal way, that you are talking from a place that sounds like there is only one truth. Is there a danger, when relating from this impersonal space, that there is a kind of pat response? Where do you go to receive your answers? Is there a way that each individual is still included in the response?

Paul: I only half heard your question. I was just feeling my love for you and realizing how happy I am about the change that has happened to you. I feel that you have let go of the personal and your pride, and that your true being is shining. I love being with you.

I'll see if I can remember your question. There is no pat response possible, because all people are so wonderfully unique, and it's the fact that they are so unique that makes them so rich, and thus the universe so rich. Each individual has gone through his own myriad of paths to reach this place.

The place we have reached at this time is so rich and wonderful because we have done so many things, which include things that have been called wrong and bad and dark.

They have all added to our richness, and so human beings at this time are the richest they have ever been. They are probably further up the path than ever before.

Now it is time to go home, this experiment is over. It is time to let go of the suffering and the struggling and to go back to the light again. Each person who sits there has just got this richness in him, and everybody is so unique that there isn't possibly a way of giving a pat response, although the words may be the same. Each independent person has to be felt, has to be seen and has to be appreciated, so there is a tuning in. As I was saying, it's a different tuning in for me now. It's not tuning in to the personal and the character, it's tuning in to a higher level of them. Then it's the same thing for everybody, be present, be aware, be truthful, be courageous, be choiceless. That's all. Each individual will hear that differently, so it has to be translated in some way. I might say to a person that he has to let go of everything instantly. The mind says, "I have to give up my job and my family and this and that." The mind clicks to the opposite extreme, so it has to be explained to this person that it's not that. I was talking about letting go of it, not getting rid of it, letting go of the attachment. Somebody else might hear something totally different, and then her mind again goes off and imagines all kinds of things. So I just say, "Come back, let go of the mind and feel what I am saying." On this other level, the higher Self is saying, "Of course I've been telling this person the same thing the whole of her life, and the life before that and the life before that."

Everybody knows everything. Everything that is contained in this universe is contained in each being. Jesus had a way of saying it, "The Kingdom of God is within." It's not just that the Kingdom of God is within, God is within. It's not just that God is within, each person is God, in a way that the mind cannot understand. So the mind will say, "Oh, so I'm God." It's not that. Everybody is Godliness now, and has never not been. But it's telling each person that, in a way that he can connect with it. The most effective way I have found of helping anybody is to see him and let him feel that he is seen, that's all.

We have all been told that we are wrong about this, we didn't do that right, we could have been more this or less that. There is all this strain because everybody who looks has a judgment about how we should be. If somebody looks and says, "I can see that about you, you are greedy." Just as a statement. Or, "You get angry a lot." Just as a statement, no judgment about it. "I've seen that part of you, that's interesting isn't it? Shall we have a look at that, do you want to talk about that?" Something relaxes. If a person is seen, he feels loved, he feels accepted. It's the art of seeing. How do we see? We have got to see ourselves first. When we see ourselves we won't like what we see, we have to take a look at that and find a way of accepting that we don't like what we see. Find a way of accepting what we see, and then through that comes a love. The moment you reach that place of love with yourself, it's with everybody.

Velusia: I have a feeling as you say that, that at that point the struggle finishes. Is that right? Is it possible that after you have worked for growth for so long, you reach a point where the struggle stops, but the movement still continues just through being honest?

Paul: There is a certain struggle needed, though struggle is really a form of resistance. It's one foot on the accelerator and one foot on the brake. It does need effort, it does need work, it does need being here, and that is hard. But, after a certain amount of work, you have to stop this because it is going away from who you are. If you are really seen by one person, your life changes. The struggle can start to diminish and you can begin to let that go.

People don't understand this, but you are perfect the way you are now. Everybody is perfect now. Nobody can understand that, "But I still overeat or I still get angry at people." With acceptance it's perfect. Then it just becomes appropriate, it changes on its own. It's just perfect, it's the attitude that makes us seem ugly, just the attitude that we have picked up.

Velusia: I have heard you talk about retiring to Australia, and when I listen to you, I feel that your art is what you are talking about right now. The way you see and love people and the way you move with that. I am wondering if that isn't your creativity and if that is something that can be stopped?

Paul: I have retired. What I have retired from is working on myself, and the moment I stopped working on myself, of course, I stopped working on everybody else. There is no difference. The reason that a sex therapist does sex therapy is because he is still involved in sex. The reason a person still does anger therapy is because he is still involved in anger.

We are all doing what we need to do in some way, whether we are leading workshops or participating in them. So, as you know, at the end I was doing meditation groups and now that's over. Life has become a meditation. It's over, I am home. There are other levels to that and I am open to them, but there is no work to do. It is just a matter of being present and being open and then what is appropriate happens. This has happened and I love sharing it when somebody is available for that. If somebody doesn't want to do that, that's perfect too, everything is perfect. I have retired so I am available.

I've spent my whole life, and lives and lives, seeking this. It's happened and I have got this to share. It's not over, there are other levels and other levels available, but I have retired from working on myself. I've retired from working on anybody else. I don't have to convince anybody now, because I know. If you are still convincing somebody, it means that you don't know. As soon as you know, you know.

Velusia: Do you have any images of yourself in retirement? Would you see yourself doing anything like gardening or potsing around in any way?

Paul: I used to do everything. I used to make my own clothes, do my own laundry and repair anything that needed to be repaired, fix the car... and now it is all fading away. It's fading away because I am finding I can't hold that level of vibration anymore. The body is vibrating at a totally different level. What it is doing is radiating the whole time. Wherever it is, it's affecting everything around. It's as though this is a radio tuner that has tuned into a higher level of frequency, so now instead of tuning into lower levels which include all the human things, it's started to tune into a much higher level and it's bringing that through.

It's a receiving station and it's bringing it to the planet. That's what happens to anybody who reaches this place. That's why meditation is so important. Not just so people can see themselves, but during that time, they bring this level to the planet, and it affects everything. So it's healing itself and it's healing the planet all the time now. Then it has an unfinished job. It made an agreement before it came here to a team of people to help them wake up to who they are, so they could go out and help people to wake up to who they are. A large number of people are needed awake at the moment, because the planet is in a transition of consciousness. The more people who are awake, the more people can take advantage of this change of vibration, and the more pleasant it will be on the planet. So, it sits and it lies and it reads occasionally. It has stopped listening to music, but somewhere it's saying, "Be available." It's available. Wherever it's called, it will go. If there is a conference it will go. If there is some person who really wants me, it will go. It's just available. So, as I say, it has retired from itself, it's retired from changing things but now it is totally available.

Velusia: What I hear you saying is, it's not your desire anymore to go out and do something. You would be available for somebody else's calling?

Paul: It is the same when people around me call me. As you know, the other day somebody in the team said, "I really want to travel with you, and be with you, I really want to be around what is happening." Then it's choiceless. If a person wants it that much, that's what happens. If some-body is around me and wants it that much, I am available, I'm here.

Then, if a person closes off, or decides she is going on a holiday from consciousness for a while, then that is what she has to do. Then I am not called, I am not needed for her in that time. When somebody's around me who wants to share what's happened to me, it's like touching a cat and the cat might like to be touched, but it loves being stroked, because that movement moves something. And that movement is blissful, it's wonderful that somebody wants to share what's happened.

It's wonderful, because in another way we are all one, and every time somebody comes home, we are all affected. Every time somebody has a realization, that's part of me that has a realization, because through this it has realized itself. Although it has come home, it is not finally home until everything and everybody is home. So, every time anybody says, "Oh yes," that's me saying that. In another way every time somebody goes, "Oh no," that's me again.

Let me say once again what I keep saying over and over. What has happened to me, has never not happened in me. It's always been here. All that happened was I woke up to the fact that this was always awake. I was asleep to the fact that it was awake. Now I know that it is the same with every single person, that whatever you call it, that light, that vibration, that love, that magnificence, God is in everybody. It has never not been in there. It's just a mat-ter of choice, a matter of intent, it's a matter of, "Do I want to find it enough?" If you do, nothing can possibly stop you. We are literally creating our existence from moment to moment. When you say, "I want to know that, I want to know myself," you'll know it. Then, when that becomes your prime intent, you'll suddenly start to hear where you need to be, what's most advantageous for you, what's most helpful for you, what's the most loving and beautiful for you. You'll hear that, you'll get drawn to it, and then you just have to have the courage to say, "Okay, let's go."

CHAPTER EIGHTEEN

BEING YOURSELF

An Interview by Salila

Salila: I wanted to talk to you today about the notion of people just being themselves. Working with you and being with you these last months, I have heard you saying again and again that all people really need to do is be present and be themselves. I realize that most of us are still somehow very afraid of that. We'd rather do a technique, even something as strong or intense as bioenergetics, rather than just be faced with the simplicity of being ourselves.

Paul: Most of the time we avoid being ourselves. That probably started when we were children, when we were told we were wrong. We were too noisy, or we made a mess, or we did things at the wrong time, or we wanted attention when our parents were tired and busy. I think we have been taught that we have got to be careful all the time, because basically we are wrong, we are all miserable sinners, we are carrying the sins of our forefathers. And so we are wrong, and somewhere that voice is thinking all the time, "I'm wrong."

Many of the masters say, "So, do this." You are in such a mess, you've got to do bioenergetics, or primal, or encounter. You've got to do something to put yourself right. I don't see that as so. I think that if a person is ready to face himself now, then all he needs to look at in himself, just surfaces on its own. But we're very lazy, and we keep looking for shortcuts. There aren't any shortcuts, but there are quick ways and slow ways. I think doing bioenergetics and cathartic stuff is the long way around.

The quick way is to be who you are, now. When you do that, all the things you have been told about yourself come up. You are not worthy, you get angry, you are not loving. They all surface, and we don't want to face them, so we go and do catharsis instead. All you need is to be who you are.

Salila: When these uncomfortable things are coming up, when you see yourself being angry, or jealous, or sexual when it's not appropriate, how can we be with that?

Paul: You know, if you have got a really heavy weight that you want to lift, and you decide to use a pulley and rope to lift it, you can use one pulley and one rope, but you have to pull very hard. However, it moves quickly because there is only one rope and one pulley. Then it might be too hard for you to do that, so you use what is called a block and tackle, and you use many pulleys and then you pull many, many times but it's easier to pull.

When you go to a therapist, it makes it easier. You can pull and pull and pull, and you don't notice how heavy the weight is, but you've got to pull for a very long time, you've got to work through things.

Being yourself is no blocks, it means that you are going to go directly to the source. Now, that can be excruciating.

The ego hates seeing who it really is, it hates seeing all the stupid things it's done. It hates seeing how unconscious it's been. So you do these therapies in order to be with somebody who says, "It's Okay. Do it this way...do it that way." And eventually you get over it. If you don't do that, you go down a vertical line.

Let's take an example, say somebody insults you. Now, everybody has a different way of handling it. Some people will completely shut off. They just go dead, nothing happens, they've gone into the cupboard. Somebody else will immediately get angry. Another person will feel sorry for himself. Everybody has a different way of handling an energy that comes across that is painful. Now, it's painful, usually because what the person says is true, not because it's untrue. If it is not true, it normally doesn't touch you. If it's true, it means he is telling you something about yourself that you don't want to know, so then you produce a number of ways of avoiding that.

Let's look at what would happen if you did not do that. First, you find the anger. If you don't do anything with that anger, you don't express it back at the other person, and you don't suppress it in yourself, you are going to find that under that there is something else, and it might mean that you are hurt.

Then you want to do something with the hurt. If you don't do anything with the hurt, you'll find there is another level to that, and there's another level below that. One of them is helplessness. If you keep going down, you come to this level of helplessness. This person has just done something, where he has brought your attention to something in yourself, that has started something off in your system that is very uncomfortable. You can't do anything about it, because once those chemicals are started, there's absolutely nothing you can do. So you've got to stay there and be with it, and we hate being helpless.

Instead, we come over the top and do something, cut off or feel sorry for ourselves. Maybe blame the person, "Who are you, anyway, to say that?" Anything, rather than just feel who we are in that moment.

Now, that is not who you are. It is what you are experiencing in that moment; so, practically, that is who you are in that moment. Not only do you have these levels of yourself, you have levels of yourself that you are not in touch with at that moment. All you need to do is feel who you are in that moment, that's all. You don't need bioenergetics, primal, encounter, breathwork or Rolfing. You don't need meditation, Vipassana or Zazen. You don't need anything, because this becomes your meditation.

Meditation is nothing else than being totally present. In fact, most meditations don't do that. They give you a mantra or they give you a breathing method which takes you away. It's nothing else but being totally present to who you are right now. That means you expand, you become sensitive, you don't contract and become insensitive. You just be who you are and experience what you are experiencing.

Salila: There seems to be a key in there that I'm not clear about yet. When you are feeling something strongly, and not acting it out on someone, and not taking it in on yourself, how can you be present with that in neutral gear?

Paul: When you say that, what you are saying is, "How do I look for the next step?" The answer is you don't. That's wanting to go beyond where you are. That's saying, "I don't want to be angry, and therefore I am going to avoid being angry."

What I am saying is, you accept your anger. Throwing it out is not accepting it, suppressing it is not being with it. If you are angry, you are angry. If you really accept that, if you don't go out there and you don't go in, if you are right with your anger and you say, "I am angry right now," you will find you are not angry. You'll find just by going right to the very source of the anger, by going into that white hot spot, it's gone.

There will be something else, and that might feel better or it might feel worse. Then you are going to have to do the same thing with that, "I don't want to feel this hurt. How can I get out of this hurt? Who are you anyway, you don't know what you are talking about?" Or, "I'm going to go back and say everybody is against me." Instead of just staying right in the middle of the hurt, "I am hurting."

So, your question says, "How do I avoid this?" I'm not saying avoid it, you don't. You don't go into the center of the anger in order for it to go. You don't know whether it's going to go or not. If you want it to go, then you are not going into the center, you are circling around trying to get rid of it. I am saying that in that moment you might be angry for the rest of your life, and it might get worse. It might get more, and more and more, but you are saying, "I am going to the center of this. I am not going to go away. I am going to experience what this anger is. If I throw it on you, I am not going to experience it. I am going to try and give it to you to deal with." The alternative is to do the opposite, "I am going to cut off from myself, I am going to pretend it's not there, I'm going to close down all my cells, close down my sensitivity." What you have to do is say, "I am angry in this moment. What is this anger? What is it?"

And then, if you are really, really there, it's gone. If you are absolutely total with it, you'll start to see what your anger is. You'll start to see that a chemical has been released in the body and you'll see what that does. You'll feel it rushing through your bloodstream and going into the muscles. You'll feel it bringing up a tension. You'll feel your head change. You'll see that your eyesight has gone a little blurred. You'll feel the whole experience of anger.

If you experience it without judgment, you'll see it is just a rush of energy. If you are trying to avoid it or you have got a judgment about it, then you'll see it as what you call anger and all the connotations that go with it.

Salila: So, lets look for a minute at what we would call normal people. One day, as it happened to me, they wake up and see, "I am not happy with the way I am living my life right now. I don't know what it is that's going on but I just know that something is not right." At that time, that's how I started. I went into primal. I wanted to work on myself. But what I understand from you is that it is not necessary to go that way. All that's needed is just to keep paying attention, staying with what is happening and somehow the next step will open up.

Paul: Let's take a look at this. When you wake up in the morning and you feel that you are not happy with the way that your life is at the moment, it is an accumulation. It is one compromise after another that you have made in your life. It is one dishonesty after another. So, your parents said, "Don't do that." So, you didn't do that, out of fear or out of wanting their approval. You didn't not do that because you didn't want to do it, you compromised at that time. You didn't just accept what they said. Maybe they said "Don't put your hand in the fire." So you didn't put your hand in the fire because they told you not to. You knew they would get angry and withdraw their love if you did. You didn't do that because you knew that was not the thing to do. You suppressed it. You suppressed one thing after another.

When you are at school, if you don't say the right things to your particular teacher, you get bad marks or get into trouble, or maybe get ridiculed in the class. You start work. You are not going to get the promotion, you are not going to earn more money, so you are compromising more and more.

What compromising is, to me, is lying. You are lying to yourself. If you are absolutely present and you say, "I am not going to do that because that person said so, and they'll punish me if I do." Then there is an awareness in that. You have taken responsibility. However, most of us don't do that. We compromise unconsciously, and that is lying. That builds up an energy in you. In fact, that is what kills most people. That is where their cancer, their heart attacks, their rheumatism and arthritis comes from. It all comes from the energy that hasn't been expressed healthily. Now, in any moment, your path to truth is open, the door never closes, but often it is in an inconvenient direction. So, you wake up in the morning and somewhere in your consciousness is exactly what you need to do. That might mean leaving your job, or your family or maybe your studies. But you are going to say, like you always do, "How can I get what I want within this situation?" In other words, you are compromising again, you are lying again. The fact is, you can't go to work everyday with this boss who is on your case, because his wife is on his case, because the children are on her case...and so on and so on. They are all passing down this energy that they don't want.

It's a good job, and it's good money and you are afraid of just setting off out into the world. So you compromise and say, "How can I be happy in this situation?" Probably you can't. I am not saying it is not possible to be open and loving in any situation. One day that can happen. But, when you start to wake up with all this contraction, it's not possible. You need to do something, but then you don't want to do it. You don't want to sell your house or leave your job. You don't want to get rid of your BMW. You want all the benefits and to be free at the same time. I am not saying that that is impossible, but for most people it's not possible. That is why they feel bad so much of the time. So, if you were to wake up in the morning and say, "I don't like the way my life is going at the moment, what do I need to do?" And you were really ready to do everything necessary, you are already out of it. It's already over, you are already free. But we don't do that. "How can I do that and not upset my wife, or my husband? How can I have it all and be free at the same time?" The answer is, at this stage, you can't.

Now, you can either go straight there and that means you just put a clean piece of paper in front of you and you say, "Okay, I have got nothing, I am attached to nothing, and nobody, in any way whatsoever. It doesn't matter that I spent seven years in a law school, or a medical school, I am not going to take it for granted that I am going into law or into medicine. I am just absolutely here and I am free. I can do anything I want to, I can go anywhere I want to." Then you are free. What happens is the higher part of your system suddenly becomes available.

If you are a doctor, it's not the part that remembers the books about diagnosis, it's the part that just flashes, "That's what's wrong with this person." It just flashes there, it doesn't work through it. If you are a lawyer, it isn't the one that remembers all the laws and all the studying, it's just the one that suddenly sees, "That's the way." It just flashes in. That part suddenly becomes available to you and it'll say, "Get out! Don't be here anymore." Or, "You just need to do this." It'll tell you exactly what to do. But only if you are conditionless. If you have got a condition, you have put a barrier in front of that, and then you put another one and another one, then it can't tell you anything. You can't hear it, because you don't want to hear it. It might say, "Get out!" And you don't want to do that, so, you don't hear it. If you wake up, and you really say, "I am ready to do anything and go anywhere," your message will be right there. It might mean you stay exactly where you are and just change your attitude. It might mean get out. But we don't do that, so, then we say, "How can I get free within this situation?" So then you have got to do bioenergetics or something else.

Salila: Got it! I am getting an image in my mind of a city such as London and a magician comes and...PUFFF! He casts an energy out to the city which creates everybody getting up in the morning and saying, "Right, I am conditionless. Here we go." What is your image of what would happen to London or a place like that, should something like that just open for everybody. Do you think everybody would move?

Paul: It's far, far away from a possibility...

Salila: Well, it's far away from a possibility now, but, if all the predicted disturbances, such as earthquakes and ecological disasters and financial disasters start to happen, it will break down all of these support systems. Sooner or later, something will be free like that, and people will start to see that the support systems aren't something to live in, then they will start moving. Do you think everyone will leave their family, stay with their family, go somewhere else, just be cast adrift, what do you see happening?

Paul: Let's just cut through. I'll tell you something else. What I am talking about is just waking up in the morning and being choiceless. You suddenly say, "I am choiceless, I don't know what is best for me, or anybody or anything." Then you look at that a little bit. Let's take a married couple who are not getting on, and fighting all the time. That's like many married couples. They have children, and what they say is, "We are not going to break up because of the children." And usually that is not true. What they are saying is, "I don't want the insecurity of that." Or, the person who is going to look after the children says, "I don't want the responsibility." It is not honest. It's usually not true. We don't know what the truth is, nobody knows what the truth is while they are in the mind.

When they move to the intuition, they are likely to flash on truth. It just beams through. But, we don't know what is best for us. We just come from the mind, and so we are scheming inside with our minds about what is best, but it all comes from a place that can't see. The computer isn't big enough to handle all that. So most of our decisions are based on something that is too small. If we were to let that go, and say, "I don't know whether it's better to keep this family together, and have the kids around two fighting adults. Maybe it's better to let it go, I don't know." If you move to, "I don't know." Something expands.

What expands is the heart. The heart doesn't expand when we are based on survival. Survival is totally selfish. Most missionaries I met when I was working in Africa were based on survival. They weren't helping people, they were taking care of number one. "This is the only way I am comfortable, by helping those people. So, you are going to be helped." It didn't come from the heart, it came from survival. "If I don't help you, I am not going to Heaven." It didn't come from an expanded place that says, "This is what I want to do for me" If you want to share that, it's beautiful. The missionaries had targets to reach, they had to have so many converts. It was survival. That is not the heart. If you come to this place of choicelessness, "I don't know." The heart expands.

When the heart expands, you start to feel a respect, an acceptance, a loving for yourself. When that happens, you don't do anything automatically. You will never pass a beggar on the street without seeing into his heart. Sometimes you might find the beggar is just on a scam, and that is his way of enjoying himself, he doesn't need the money. Sometimes you'll find that this person is really suffering. But you will see each person, you will see each cat, each dog, each child, each leaf. You will see, and when you see, you love. It's not a doing, you don't constantly think, "I love you." Love is just there. As soon as that happens, everything becomes appropriate. So you might say, "If this magician waves his wand over London, then there will be no taxis and nobody can go anywhere." But, if the taxi driver opens up, he'll say, "Do I want to drive my taxi today?" Then he might get in contact with these people who want to go to places and he'll say, "I'd love to do that!"

Then you will have a totally different taxi driver. You'll have somebody who just loves driving a taxi, doing it for the love of it and not out of survival.

Certainly, there would be a huge shift, because if people wake up, they'll become honest. That is the basis of everything we have talked about today. It's being honest. Are you honest with yourself? Are you honest with the other? Honesty has all these levels. "Yes, of course I want to do this because I've got to keep my kids in food and I need to look after my family and... yes, of course".

Look under there and you might find another level. Keep looking and you will find levels and levels. When you come to the bottom, you will be love. Not loving, but everything you do will be love. You will never unconsciously grab a door handle again, you won't throw your shoes down, you will never be careless with your clothes. You will realize everything has a consciousness. Everything. You will treat everything beautifully and naturally. You will take care, and then out of this openness that happens in you comes a response. You no longer do anything, you respond to a situation.

So you are walking past the beggar and you look, or you sense. When you are really open, you don't have to look because you sense, and you will know whether this person needs money or not, and if he does, how much. You will respond choicelessly. Maybe you give him your last ten dollars because you know that he needs it more than you. You won't worry at all. You will know you are being taken care of. When you are open, everything you need comes to you. You might feel that this person is just on a scam and he doesn't need the money. You will know that. When I say know, it is nothing active, you don't have to say, "Do they need the money or not?" You don't have to have anything at all. It is just happening inside you, it is a response. You will respond to everything and everybody around you and then that helps them to respond to you.

Salila: When you were speaking just now about the heart and people living from this expansion of the heart, I was touched by the gentleness of that. I was wondering if you have anything to say to people who are wanting to move into that expansion, into that gentleness of living that way.

Paul: We are living on a very brutal planet. It wasn't always like this. We have created it this way. A cat is a very beautiful creature but it can be savage, it kills in a very cruel way. We talk about mother nature in an affectionate way, but mother nature is generally very cruel, too. It is just one killing another. We often talk about going back to nature, but nature is very brutal and a lot of nature is absolutely violent. It doesn't kill to eat, it kills for the fun of it. This is a very gross planet to be on. We have chosen this, we created it so we could learn to dichotomize everything and see it more clearly.

When everything is one, we are actually unconscious about our consciousness. To look at it we need to separate it. Now the experiment is over, we have done that and we need to start coming out again, and so we are living in an atmosphere where it is very difficult to be loving, because there is no support. The only supports we have are the higher levels, which we are not in touch with anymore. Occasionally, somebody who has reached that place, such as a Jesus or a Buddha comes along, but the encouragement to get there is nonexistent.

We talk about the horrors of wars, how terrible they are, and the majority of people know that, but the generals and the soldiers don't, because if they did, they would not be there. They are there because they want to be violent. Most policemen do their job because they want to be violent, not because they want peace. They don't even realize that there is violence in them. People watch violent movies because it is a violent planet we live on and the majority of movies today have violence in them.

We keep saying it is out there, outside of ourselves. It is not out there, it is in each and every one of us, without exception. This dimension is violent and that is in Jesus and Buddha too. With awareness, with awakening, with choicelessness, we acknowledge that violence. When you are really open you say, "I could easily jump on this person. I could easily kill him, but I don't need to go there." And then slowly, as that goes, love naturally emerges.

Most people who are talking about stopping wars are at war in themselves the whole time. They are at war at work, where they are trying to do better than their competitors. They are trying to beat somebody else in their offices to the better jobs and when they get home they are at war with their partners. But these are merely symptoms that came from everybody being at war with himself. People don't accept themselves, they don't love themselves.

If you don't accept and love yourself, you will never love anybody else. You might get infatuated, you might get a sentimental feeling for somebody, but you cannot love anyone else until you have learned to love yourself. That's because you don't know what it is. You think it is outside yourself, but you have to find it inside. Whenever you feel anything, it is you whom you are feeling, not the other. We are living in a violent place and that is because of unacceptance. We just need to start to accept, "This is the way I am, this is what I am doing." If you don't do anything with it, you will start to see pieces more clearly. As you see it, it will start to move into another layer and then another layer, and as you keep following these layers you will reach your higher Self, your light, God or whatever name you like to give it. You will reach a place of total purity.

Some see it as light, some see it as darkness, some see it as God. If you see it as anything, then you haven't reached the bottom. When you have reached the bottom, it is just pure "isness." We can call it love, but to call it love, is just a contamination. It is just a gentleness, a sensitivity, a caring that is natural, that flows. To get to that place, each of us has to look at himself, not anybody else, not looking at how we can change the politicians or the generals, because we can't until we have realized that place in ourselves.

The moment you have realized that place in yourself, you realize it in another. As soon as you have found this place of love in yourself, you realize the place of love in another, and you commune with that person in a totally different way. That communion helps him to see that part in himself. If enough people are genuinely looking at themselves, then as each person blossoms the whole of the planet is affected. In fact, the whole of the universe is affected. It looks impossible because up until now it has taken twenty years or thirty lifetimes for people to realize themselves. We have that conditioning in us, but it is not true any more because the experiment is over.

The experiment was to make it hard so you had to work your way home. And on your way home you learned things, you experienced things which the rest of the universe could benefit from. The experiment is now over, the struggle on earth is over, the light is here. All we have to do is wake up to that. We are so caught in our darkness, we think we have to work through everything and if you think it hard enough, you have to do that. It's over, the light is here, the realms are here. What we call angels and ascended masters and ascended beings, are all pouring to this place at the moment and saying,

"It is over, come back home now. Just let go of that place you needed to be in as a part of the experiment. Let go and fly back home on your own."

The struggle is over.

Paul is available to speak and share his
insight and vision at meetings,
conferences and seminars.
For details of his itinerary and availability
please contact the publishers.

Most of the interviews in this book are available on
Audio and Video Cassettes
and can be obtained by mailorder from the publishers.
For catalogs and further information:

The Roximillion Publications Corporation
1202 Lexington Avenue
Suite 325
New York, NY 10028